TIME
for KiDS

HEROES
of
BLACK
HISTORY

Published by Liberty Street, an imprint of
Time Inc. Books
225 Liberty Street
New York, NY 10281

ISBN: 978-1-68330-012-0
Library of Congress Control Number: 2017944228

First edition, 2017
1 QGT 17
10 9 8 7 6 5 4 3 2 1

We welcome your comments and suggestions about Time Inc. Books. Please write to us at:

Time Inc. Books
Attention: Book Editors
P.O. Box 62310
Tampa, FL 33662-2310
(800) 765-6400

timeincbooks.com

Time Inc. Books products may be purchased for business or promotional use. For information on bulk purchases, please contact Christi Crowley in the Special Sales Department at (845) 895-9858.

Some material for this book was derived from other sources; they are listed on page 192.

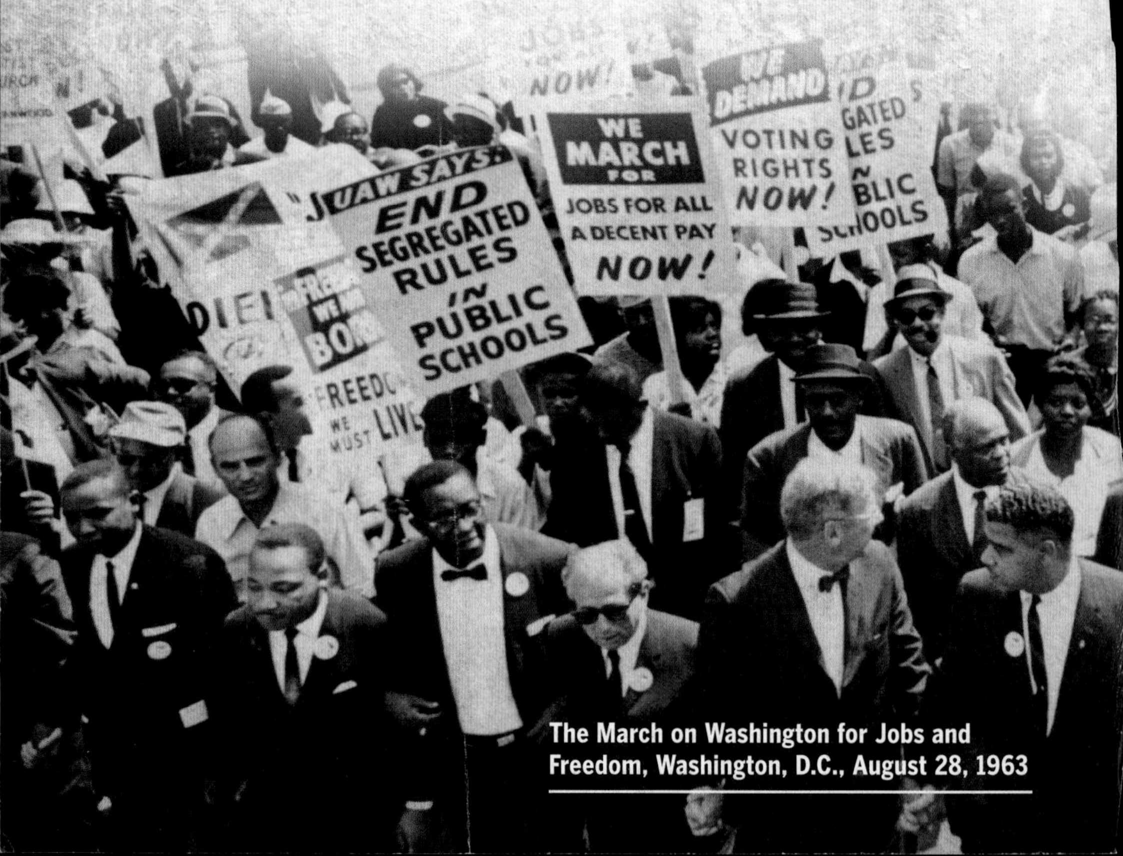

The March on Washington for Jobs and Freedom, Washington, D.C., August 28, 1963

TIME
for KiDS

HEROES
of
BLACK HISTORY

Biographies of Four Great Americans

By the editors of TIME FOR KIDS Magazine

With an introduction by Charlayne Hunter-Gault

Contents

Jackie Robinson, 1945

Introduction

I t's been a long time since I was a child, but history lessons I learned back then have followed me throughout my life. They helped me navigate places where, initially, the color of my skin kept me out and created challenges. It was history—what I call my "invisible armor"—that enabled me to meet those challenges and realize my dreams.

At my all-black high school in Atlanta, Georgia, my fellow students and I were inspired by many black freedom fighters, including Henry McNeal Turner, a hero from an earlier time for whom our school was named. And one of the heroes in our own time, Rosa Parks, helped inform us as we challenged separate and unequal places in the late 1950s and early '60s. Rosa Parks was the mother of the freedom movement. She helped her "children" in Atlanta and all over the South move it closer to freedom and justice for all.

My armor enabled me to face hostile white mobs who yelled ugly words at me, and the rock thrown through my dormitory window, when I was entering the University of Georgia. That armor was created in part by the history of giants like Harriet Tubman, whose commitment to freedom and justice for all led her on missions far more dangerous than mine.

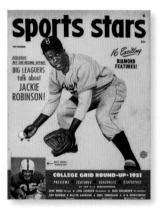

Hamilton Holmes, the classmate who entered the University of Georgia with me, shared more than a few traits with Jackie Robinson. Hamilton came from an athletic family, and I have no doubt that Jackie Robinson's breakthrough as the first African American to play Major League Baseball was an inspiration to them. Hamilton was an athlete himself, but the lessons passed on to him through greats like Robinson also had an impact on his demeanor. Even when he was yelled at with harsh, racist words, Hamilton never shouted back or reacted. He was always calm, cool, and collected, and despite the ugly distractions went on to graduate with the distinction of Phi Beta Kappa, the institution's highest academic honor.

It's important to know our history, not just for people who look like me, but for all people who want to be good citizens. For generations—even before the adoption of the Constitution—there have been people who have invested their time and energy in seeing to it that every human being in this country enjoys freedom, justice, and equality.

We can all learn from Barack Obama, who said, when he was running for president the first time, "I stand on the shoulders of giants." He, too, wore the armor his white mother gave him, all the way to the White House. And there were many other white people who helped in our stride toward freedom.

We have indeed taken amazing strides toward realizing the promise of our Constitution, but we all still need to be vigilant. That means staying true to our country's promise, as demonstrated in the examples of the people whose stories are contained in this book. Remembering times when there were challenges to our better selves, or our freedoms, philosopher George Santayana once warned, "Those who cannot remember the past are condemned to repeat it."

We have a great country, despite its challenges, and it will be up to the generation reading this book to use its lessons to keep it that way— knowing that regardless of race, creed, or color, they, like these heroes of black history, are protected by history's armor.

Charlayne Hunter-Gault
2017

In 1961, Charlayne Hunter was one of two black students to enter the all-white University of Georgia. Along with her high school classmate Hamilton Holmes, Charlayne fought, and won, a legal battle to be admitted to a school that had educated only white students for almost two centuries. Many white students at the university did not want African Americans to attend. Charlayne and Hamilton were frequently harassed by students and even by police. A riot broke out outside Charlayne's first-floor dorm room one night, and

Charlayne Hunter (center) and Hamilton Holmes (right center) are mobbed by reporters on the grounds of the University of Georgia, January 1961.

someone threw a rock through her window. Charlayne and Hamilton were even suspended from school for a time—"for their own safety," as school officials put it.

Charlayne—later assuming her married name, Hunter-Gault—went on to become a successful journalist and correspondent, and worked for the *New Yorker* magazine, the *New York Times*, the *PBS NewsHour*, National Public Radio, and CNN. She has also written three books.

Black History in America

1600s–1750

Slaves are brought to America

Most black Americans can trace their roots to western Africa. From the 1500s to the mid-1800s, Europeans shipped about 12 million black slaves from Africa to the United States and Europe. The first black African slaves in America arrived during the early 1600s, when slavery based on race became a way of life in all 13 colonies. By 1750, about 200,000 slaves lived in the colonies.

1800–1865

A movement to end slavery

By the early 1800s, most northern states had taken steps to abolish, or end, slavery. During the mid-1800s, abolitionists began to enter politics and use their homes to help black slaves escape to the North. This was called the **Underground Railroad.** Harriet Tubman, a runaway slave herself, helped about 300 blacks escape to freedom.

1865–1872

Road to freedom

Slavery was outlawed by the **13th Amendment,** ratified on December 6, 1865. Earlier that year, Congress had established the Freedmen's Bureau to help former slaves resettle into life. Despite its accomplishments, the Freedmen's Bureau did not solve the serious economic problems of black Americans. Most continued to live in poverty. In 1865 and 1866, many southern state governments passed restrictive laws that became known as the black codes. The black codes shocked a powerful group of northern congressmen called the Radical Republicans. They worked hard to pass the **14th Amendment,** which gave citizenship to black Americans. It also guaranteed that all federal and state laws would apply equally to everyone, regardless of race. In the 1890s, however, a series of laws passed throughout the South, known as Jim Crow laws, imposed rules that segregated, or separated, white citizens from black citizens.

1905–1909

The NAACP is formed

In 1905, the **Niagara Movement** was founded by a group of black scholars and teachers led by W.E.B. Du Bois. The scholars met near Niagara Falls in Ontario, Canada, to pass resolutions, or formal statements, demanding full equality. Du Bois went on to found the National Association for the Advancement of Colored People (NAACP) in New York City with Ida B. Wells, Mary White Ovington, and others. The NAACP's goals were to ensure the political, educational, social, and economic equality of minority citizens. Today, the NAACP is the nation's largest and best-known civil rights organization.

1920s

The Harlem Renaissance

During the 1920s, many black artists, poets, writers, and musicians moved to Harlem, a section of New York City, where they became well known for their writing, art, and music. Today, this period in history is called the **Harlem Renaissance**. During this time, black artists, such as Zora Neale Hurston, were able to open the public's eyes about the experience of being black in America. It was called a renaissance, or rebirth, because African Americans took their pain and suffering and successfully turned them into art.

1930s–1940s

Breaking barriers

In the decades leading up to the birth of the civil rights movement, many black people broke through color barriers. In 1936, Jesse Owens won four gold medals at the **Olympics in Berlin, Germany**. In 1947, Jackie Robinson played his first game with the Brooklyn Dodgers, becoming the first black player in the modern major leagues.

1950s

Fighting for civil rights

During the 1950s, black leaders began to use marches, demonstrations, and the courts to defeat racist laws. Their efforts are known as the **civil rights movement**. The most famous court case of the civil rights movement began in 1950 when 7-year-old Linda Brown of Topeka, Kansas, was denied access to a school that was just four blocks from her home because she was black. On May 17, 1954, the U.S. Supreme Court ruled in *Brown v. Board of Education* that segregation in public schools (having separate schools for white and black students) violated the Constitution.

On December 1, 1955, another important civil rights milestone occurred. Rosa Parks was arrested after refusing to give up her bus seat to a white person. Black leaders urged black people to boycott, or refuse to use, the buses in Montgomery, Alabama. A young minister named Dr. Martin Luther King, Jr., led the peaceful protest. The **Montgomery bus boycott** lasted 381 days. People walked many miles to work or home to avoid using the buses. In 1956, the U.S. Supreme Court finally ruled that

Montgomery could no longer have a segregated public transportation system because it violated the Constitution.

1960s

March on Washington

On August 28, 1963, the civil rights movement reached its height with a huge march in Washington, D.C. The **March on Washington** attracted more than 200,000 people to the Lincoln Memorial. At the march, Dr. Martin Luther King, Jr., delivered his famous **"I Have a Dream" speech**. In it, he said: "I have a dream that my four little children will one day live in a nation where they will not be judged by the color of their skin but by the content of their character."

After the march, King and other civil rights leaders met with President John F. Kennedy and Vice President Lyndon Johnson in the White House. A year later, Johnson, who became president after Kennedy was assassinated, signed the **Civil Rights Act of 1964** into law. The law guaranteed equal rights for black Americans in employment, voting, and the use of public facilities. In 1965, the **Voting Rights Act** ended racist laws that required black voters to pay a special tax or take a reading test before voting. The new law increased black voter registration throughout the South, especially in Mississippi.

1968

Year of change

On April 4, 1968, Dr. Martin Luther King, Jr., who many think of as the most important leader of the civil rights movement, was shot and killed in Memphis, Tennessee, at the age of 39. A week of rioting in at least 125 cities across the nation followed King's death. A second bill, the **Civil Rights Act of 1968,** which guaranteed the right to equal housing, was signed.

1972

Taking affirmative action

In 1972, Congress passed two key laws that helped expand job opportunities to black workers. Called **affirmative action** laws, they required governments and public institutions to hire more members of minority groups and women to help alleviate discrimination against these citizens. Since the laws were passed, there has been a huge increase in the numbers of women and minorities in all areas of employment.

1995

The Million Man March

On October 16, 1995, the Nation of Islam and its controversial leader, Louis Farrakhan, organized the **Million Man March.** At least 400,000 people, mostly black men and boys, participated in the march. The Reverend Jesse Jackson, the poet Maya Angelou, and Rosa Parks, "the mother of the civil rights movement," made speeches at the march. They spoke about the unfairness still faced by black men in this country. They also urged black men to be leaders in their communities and to work together to improve life for all black Americans. The march was repeated in years that followed, changing its name to the Million Family March and including women.

November 4, 2008

Achieving power in government

November 4, 2008, will be forever remembered as a day change came to the nation. American voters went to the polls and gave **Barack Obama** a resounding victory. He won more votes than any candidate in U.S. history. His popularity was proven once again as almost 2 million people braved frigid temperatures on the National Mall to witness history on January 20, 2009, when Obama officially became the **first African-American president of the United States.**

2013–present

A rallying cry

Despite gains in many areas, black Americans often still face discrimination and bias. Black citizens are more likely than white citizens to be arrested, and far more likely than white people to be sent to prison for the same crimes. In 2013, a man named George Zimmerman was found not guilty after shooting and killing Trayvon Martin, an unarmed black teenager. In response, Patrisse Cullors, Opal Tometi, and Alicia Garza began the **Black Lives Matter** movement. The phrase became a rallying cry for protesters in response to a series of police killings of black citizens.

Another flash point for racial tension in the United States proved to be the removal of statues of Confederate figures from public places in the South. In 2017, white supremacists, including neo-Nazis and members of the Ku Klux Klan, held a rally in Charlottesville, Virginia, that turned violent. Many were injured—and one woman was killed—as the protesters clashed with counterprotesters. It was clear that America still had a long way to go to achieve true equality.

Harriet Tubman

A Woman of Courage

DETERMINED
to be FREE

Harriet Tubman was born a slave. But she made up her mind that she would not die a slave. With courage and determination, Harriet bravely won her own freedom—and the freedom of hundreds of other slaves.

When she died at the age of 93, Harriet Tubman was a famous and respected American. The former slave risked her life many times to help other people become free. She also served her country during the Civil War as a spy and a scout. In her later years, she opened her home to people in need. She asked for nothing for herself in return.

No one knows exactly when Harriet was born. It was probably around 1820 near Bucktown, Maryland.

Harriet Tubman

Slave ships carried people from Africa to the United States. The trip was terrible, with little food, water, or air.

Slave traders had captured Harriet's grandparents in West Africa. Her parents, Harriet Green and Ben Ross, were born as slaves. So when Harriet and her brothers and sisters were born, they were slaves, too. Her parents named her Araminta. But people called her by her mother's name, Harriet.

A Hard Life

Harriet, her parents, and her eight brothers and sisters lived and worked on the Brodess plantation near Bucktown. Plantations were large farms where slaves usually did all the work. Because Harriet was a slave, her childhood was much more work than play. She started to work when she was just 5 years old. She was hired out to a nearby plantation to care for the owner's baby. When she was 6, she learned to weave and make clothes. As a young teen, she labored in the fields of corn, potatoes, and tobacco. Harriet was strong. She was very good at her jobs. But Harriet was also independent and rebellious in nature. This made her owners very angry. They would punish her with beatings.

Slave Children

Children began to work when they were young—usually 5 or 6 years old. They'd start out by looking after younger children, running errands, gathering firewood, or helping with planting. As they got older, they would get more and harder work to do. They would rake, hoe, clear weeds, and pick crops such as cotton. Some children also learned skills, such as weaving or cooking.

Like all slaves, children were property that could be sold at any time. Families were separated when slave owners sold a parent or a child. Once separated, children would usually never see their parents again.

Helping Others

One evening when Harriet was 13, she was harvesting crops with a group of other slaves. One of the men left to go to the village store. Because he didn't have permission, the overseer followed him. (An overseer was a person who was in charge of slaves.) Harriet followed, too. The overseer caught up with the man and threatened to whip him. The overseer told Harriet to help him hold the man down. She refused.

It made Harriet very angry to see people beaten. In the confusion, the man tried to run away. As the overseer tried to stop him, Harriet blocked the way. The overseer picked up a heavy weight and threw it at the man, but it hit Harriet in the head instead. Part of her skull was crushed, and she crumpled to the ground.

It took a very long time for Harriet to feel better. For the rest of her life, she had blackouts because of the injury. Harriet would suddenly fall into

Harriet always wanted to help others. Even as a teen, she stood up to adults.

a deep sleep. Then she would wake up just as suddenly and go on as though nothing had happened.

After Harriet became strong enough to work again, she went back to the fields. She drove oxen. She plowed the ground. She chopped wood and carried logs. She could do just about any job a man could do. She also learned a lot about the woods from her father—information that would come in handy later.

Harriet learned something else as well. She saw friends and family members work all day from sunrise until sunset. She saw them cruelly beaten. Harriet hated slavery, and she began to dream of a different life for herself and her family.

Slaves worked long hours. Here, slaves work in a plantation field.

MAKING HER WAY ALONE

When Harriet was in her twenties, much of her life changed. She married John Tubman, a free African-American man who lived near the plantation. But even though Harriet married a free man, she didn't become free, too. Under the law, she was still a slave, so she still had to work for the family who owned her. The only change was that Harriet was allowed to spend nights at her husband's cabin.

Harriet wondered how long she and her husband would be together. After all, the owners of the plantation could sell her at any time. Harriet had heard rumors that they were going to do just that.

Harriet was heartbroken. "I prayed all night long," she later wrote. Soon, she realized she had to do something. She wanted to stay with her family. She told John she

Slaves were kept in jail-like cells before they were sold.

wanted to run away from the Brodess plantation. She was eager to go north and be free. Most northern states did not allow slavery. If a slave escaped to one of those states, she became free. But John Tubman didn't like the idea. It would be dangerous. Also, there was a good chance that they'd be caught and beaten. He told Harriet to forget about leaving.

Harriet stopped talking to her husband about her plan. But she didn't forget about it. In fact, the more she thought about it, the more Harriet knew that she wanted to leave. She wanted to go with her husband. But if he refused to go, she would seek her freedom alone.

Harriet tried to persuade her husband to escape to the North. He decided not to go. Harriet went without him.

Planning the Escape

By 1849, Harriet was sure that she would soon be sold to another owner, far away—and farther away from the North. Harriet knew she had to leave before it was too late. She didn't tell her husband she was going, because she thought he would try to stop her. Instead, she got in touch with people who lived outside the plantation and could help her. She secretly made her plans to escape.

One night, Harriet and two of her brothers snuck out of their cabins. They ran into the nearby woods and followed a path away from the plantation. But before long, Harriet's brothers changed their minds. They knew how difficult it would be to get away. They knew they would be beaten if they were caught. So the two men decided to go back before someone came looking for them. But Harriet refused to return. She told them she would go on by herself.

Without her brothers to help and protect her, Harriet was afraid. She was a young woman, alone in the forest. How would she get food? And how did someone get to the North? She didn't know the way.

Afraid but determined, Harriet set out by herself for the free northern state of Pennsylvania. Her brothers turned back because they were afraid they'd be caught.

ON *the* WAY *to* FREEDOM

Harriet had directions to the house of a woman who would help on the first part of her journey. But Harriet didn't know this person. Could it be a trap? What if the slave hunters were waiting for her there? She could imagine the beating she would get from her owners if she was dragged back. Harriet tried to forget her fears as she walked on.

Harriet reached the home of the woman who had promised to help her. She saw that she did not have to worry. The kind woman was part of the Underground Railroad, a network of people who helped slaves escape.

Harriet was tired, thirsty, and very hungry. The woman gave her food and water. Then she told Harriet to climb into a waiting wagon. Harriet lay down, hidden by a burlap bag and vegetables. She was driven to another secret location. These kind people helped Harriet and many other slaves find freedom.

Follow Your Star

When Harriet was lucky, she got rides for short distances. But most of the time she walked. She took lonely back roads and sheltered paths

People helped Harriet find food and shelter as she traveled north to freedom.

through the woods by night, following the North Star. Along the way, strangers who were part of the Underground Railroad network helped her. Sometimes they gave Harriet food and hid her during the day. Then they gave her directions to the next place where she could get help. She crossed from Maryland into

Delaware. Then she walked north into the free state of Pennsylvania.

Harriet walked almost 100 miles from her home to freedom in Pennsylvania. When she reached the state, she headed for Philadelphia. She got a job there as a

The Underground Railroad

The Underground Railroad wasn't a real railroad with tracks and trains. It was a network of people and routes—on land and over water—that helped slaves escape from the South in the mid-1800s.

Thousands of people in cities, villages, and farm areas of the United States, Canada, and Mexico were part of the network. "Conductors" were people who helped the runaways. "Stations" were places such as attics, cellars, or overgrown areas in forests where slaves could hide. Most conductors on the Underground Railroad were African Americans who lived in the North. But whites and others became part of the network, too.

Safe houses like this one offered escaped slaves places to hide.

dishwasher and cook. Harriet also met abolitionists—people who wanted to end the practice of slavery.

The abolitionists told her many details about how the Underground Railroad worked. This would help Harriet on the dangerous missions to come.

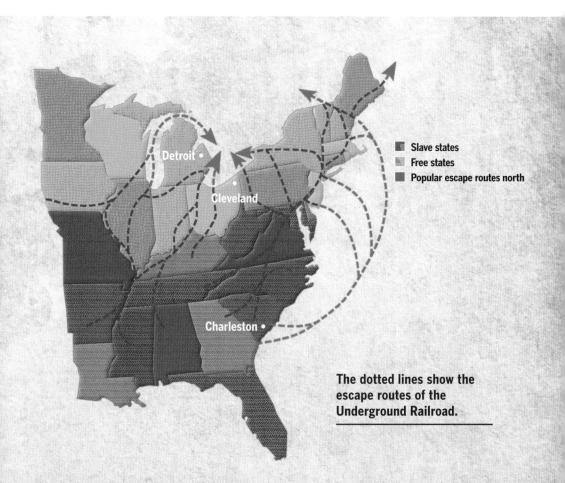

Slave states
Free states
Popular escape routes north

Detroit
Cleveland
Charleston

The dotted lines show the escape routes of the Underground Railroad.

The stakes were high: if escaping slaves were caught, they'd be dragged back to their owners and punished. But as many as 100,000 slaves managed to escape to freedom on the railroad between the 1830s and the end of the Civil War.

WORKING *on* *the* RAILROAD

Harriet loved being free. For the first time in her life, people paid her for her work. She had her own place to live. She could come and go as she pleased. But she thought about her family a lot. She missed them and wanted them to be free, too. She wanted them to be with her.

In 1850, Harriet decided to go back to Maryland to free her family. Her decision took great courage because she was a runaway slave. Once Harriet returned to Maryland, anyone could capture her and send her back to her owners.

A Dangerous Journey

Harriet returned to the Brodess plantation, where she had lived, and took the first members of her family north—a sister and her children. They walked by night and hid by day. Along the way, conductors of the Underground Railroad helped them. Harriet made several trips back to Maryland over the next few years. On one trip, she went back for her husband, but he had married someone else and did not want to leave. Harriet brought many of her brothers and sisters and their families north to freedom.

Harriet became famous for her work as a conductor on the Underground Railroad. She helped her family, and she helped many others, too. Harriet made 19 trips to the South between 1850 and 1860 to lead 300 slaves to freedom. In the 1850s, Maryland slave owners offered rewards that added up to $40,000 for her capture. No one ever caught her.

Bringing slaves to freedom was

100 DOLLARS REWARD!

Runaway from the subscriber on the 27th of July, my Black Woman, named

EMILY,

Seventeen years of age, well grown, black color, has a whining voice. She took with her one dark calico and one blue and white dress, a red corded gingham bonnet; a white striped shawl and slippers. I will pay the above reward if taken near the Ohio river on the Kentucky side, or THREE HUNDRED DOLLARS, if taken in the State of Ohio, and delivered to me near Lewisburg, Mason County, Ky.   THO'S. H. WILLIAMS.
August 4, 1853.

Slave owners offered rewards for the return of runaway slaves.

dangerous and hard. Once an owner discovered that a slave was missing, men with guns went out to search for the runaway. The slave hunters patrolled the roads and searched buildings. Slaves who were caught were severely punished. Most slaves tried several times before they finally reached freedom. Some never made it at all.

Runaway slaves and the people who helped them had to be clever to avoid capture. First, they tried to get a long head start when they escaped. That meant escaping when slave owners wouldn't miss them right away. Most slaves escaped on a holiday or a weekend. Harriet often took slaves away from plantations on a Saturday night. Most slaves did not have to work on Sundays, so their owners wouldn't miss them and wouldn't start searching until Monday.

It was important to keep plans and movements secret. Escaping slaves usually traveled at night. During the day, they hid in the woods and fields or other shelters provided by the people of the Underground Railroad. Sometimes Harriet would hide her "passengers," then check to see if it was safe for them to come out to get food, clothing, or rest at a station on the way. She might knock at the door of a house that was known as a station on the Underground Railroad. Perhaps the person inside would ask,

Slaves had to hide from slave hunters. They often found shelter and food in Underground Railroad stations.

Sojourner Truth

Sojourner Truth was born into slavery in rural New York State in 1797. In 1826, she escaped to freedom with her infant daughter. In 1828, after slaves in New York were freed, Sojourner Truth moved to New York City to begin a long career as an abolitionist and women's rights activist. She spent 40 years of her life preaching a message of equality for all people. In 1851, she delivered a famous speech called "Ain't I a Woman?" at a women's rights convention in Akron, Ohio.

"Who is there?" Then Harriet might answer, "A friend with a friend." That would let the person know that she had runaway slaves with her. Once she knew the way was clear, Harriet returned with her passengers.

Staying Safe

Runaways did what they could to hide from people who hunted them. Slave hunters often tracked slaves with dogs. The dogs' sharp sense of smell helped them find the slaves. The slaves sometimes poured pepper on their trail to confuse the dogs or walked through water to hide their scent. Some slaves didn't head north right away. They hid near home until the people who were looking for them stopped looking. Then the slaves started their journey.

A TOUGH LEADER

Harriet Tubman succeeded because she was a very tough leader. Once she started north with a group of passengers, no one was allowed to turn back. She knew that slaves who turned back might get caught. Then officials might force them to give away the locations of other runaways and people who helped them. Harriet always carried a gun with her. If someone wanted to go back, she said she'd shoot. She never did. But her words were enough to keep people moving.

Harriet and her passengers had many close calls. On one rescue trip, slave hunters were close behind her. They caught up with her and her passengers near a train station. Harriet had to think quickly. She pushed her passengers onto a train heading south.

Slaves sometimes hid in wooded areas. They watched out for slave hunters.

She knew the slave hunters would never look on that train. After all, runaway slaves wanted to go north, not south. The trick worked perfectly, and the authorities paid no attention to them.

Rescue Mission

On another mission, Harriet was back in Bucktown, Maryland, to pick up members of her family. She had just bought some live chickens at the market when she

Harriet Tubman avoided capture by setting her chickens free. The chickens made so much noise no one paid attention to Harriet!

suddenly saw her former owner walking toward her. If he saw her, her days as a free woman were over. She quickly dropped the chickens. As they squawked and flapped their wings, she turned her back and bent over to catch them. Her former owner walked right past her.

In 1857, Harriet made her most difficult journey—to get her parents. By this time, they were old and could not walk very far. Harriet had to drive them in a wagon through the states of Maryland and Delaware. A big wagon was difficult to hide and made it more likely that someone would stop them. Despite this, Harriet succeeded. She brought her parents from Maryland all the way to freedom in Canada, where she had been living. The family then moved to the small town of Auburn, in New York State. Harriet and her parents settled in a small house.

Harriet made her last trip south before the Civil War in December of 1860. She brought seven people north to freedom. Harriet Tubman was among the greatest Underground Railroad leaders that we know of. She was proud of her accomplishments. "I never lost one passenger," she said.

Harriet brought her parents to freedom in a wagon like this.

Talking in Code

People who worked on the Underground Railroad faced penalties if they were caught helping escaped slaves. And if the escaping slaves were captured, they would be sent back to their owners and severely punished. To avoid detection, Underground Railroad conductors developed a secret lingo.

Agents were people who helped plan escapes and made connections between escaped slaves and railroad conductors.

Escaped slaves traveling on the railroad were referred to as **passengers, baggage, cargo, fleece,** or **freight.** When slaves were hidden under produce in wagons, they were called a **load of potatoes.**

When conductors were waiting for escaped slaves to arrive, they called the fugitives **bundles of wood** or **parcels.**

Canada and free states in the North were called **Canaan, Heaven,** or **the promised land.**

Safe places where fugitives could hide along the railroad were called **stations** or **depots.** The people who ran them were **stationmasters.**

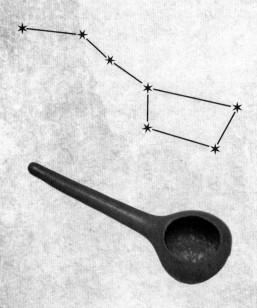

Escaped slaves were told to look for the Big Dipper, a constellation that points to the North Star. The North Star leads reliably north throughout the year. Slaves referred to the Big Dipper as the **Drinking Gourd.** A dipper is a kitchen utensil also called a ladle or scoop. Before modern plumbing, people working outdoors would get drinks from buckets of water using dippers. Sometimes dippers were hollowed-out gourds.

THE CIVIL
WAR YEARS

By 1860, Harriet Tubman was well known for her daring slave rescues. She made speeches against slavery at abolitionist meetings. She also spoke to support the struggle for women's rights. During Harriet's lifetime, women did not have the same rights as men.

Harriet's life was about to change once again. In early 1861, a huge problem was growing in the United States. The slave states and the free states disagreed about whether slavery should be allowed in the new western territories. Abraham Lincoln was against the spread of slavery to the West. When he was elected president in November 1860, the slave states feared that he would end slavery. From 1860 to 1861, 11 southern slave states separated from the United States,

A Confederate flag is raised over Fort Sumter the day after the fort was taken by Confederate soldiers.

which became known as the Union. They formed a separate country called the Confederate States of America. In April 1861, Confederate soldiers attacked the Union's Fort Sumter in South Carolina. The Civil War had begun.

A Hard Decision

When the Civil War started, Harriet helped the Union. It was a hard decision for her. Her parents lived with her and she took care of them. Who would care for them if she left? Harriet decided that she had to go to war. The cause of the Union was too important. When Harriet was gone, people in Auburn helped care for her mother and father.

During the Civil War, Harriet did many jobs to help others. She worked as a nurse and cook for the Union. Harriet was also a valuable scout and spy. She knew how to survive in forests and swamps. She often went behind enemy lines in the South and gained the trust of slaves there. They gave her important information about the locations of Confederate supplies and Confederate soldiers. She took that information back to the Union army. Harriet also led a group of former slaves who spied on the Confederate States.

About 134,000 freed slaves fought for the Union in the Civil War.

Harriet led Union soldiers through enemy territory as a scout. In 1863, she led a group of 150 African-American soldiers on a raid up the Combahee River in South Carolina. They destroyed Confederate supplies and crops and freed about 800 slaves.

Harriet also worked in army hospitals. She took care of injured soldiers. She bathed them and cleaned their wounds. Some of her homemade remedies, made from local plants and roots, helped ease the fever and suffering of sick soldiers.

Harriet baked pies and gingerbread and made root beer at night in her tiny cabin. A friend sold the goodies at army camps to help Harriet support herself.

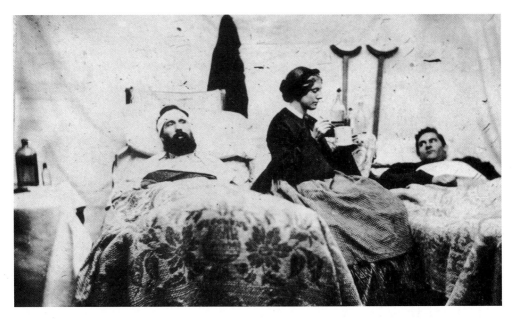

Civil War soldiers are cared for by a nurse in a military hospital. Harriet Tubman might have worked in a hospital much like this.

Harriet often passed on information she had learned from slaves to Union spies.

The army didn't have records of Harriet's work, so she didn't get a salary.

When the Civil War ended in 1865, Harriet returned to her home in Auburn, New York. During the four-year struggle, she had helped in the fight to keep the Union together—and to end slavery. She had helped make the lives of sick and wounded soldiers a bit better. She had risked her life to fight for freedom for all people. But Harriet knew that there was still much more work to be done.

Now it was time to help others closer to home.

HARRIET'S LATER YEARS

Harriet was happy to be back home in Auburn with her parents. But Harriet was poor. She had spent her whole life helping others, and she had very little money. Without proper records of her work during the war, the U.S. government wouldn't give her money for it. She still owed money to a bank for the house she shared with her mother and father. Now the bank said it would take Harriet's house if she could not pay back the money she owed.

A writer named Sarah Bradford heard about Harriet's problem. Sarah admired Harriet for her courage and hard work. Harriet had helped many people, and now Sarah wanted to help her. Harriet agreed to let Sarah

Harriet posed for this photograph while living in Auburn, New York.

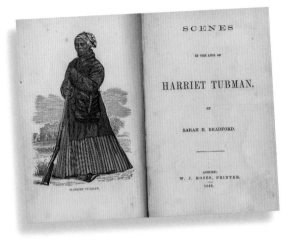

The title page from *Scenes in the Life of Harriet Tubman* by Sarah Bradford

write a book about her life. The book told the amazing story of Harriet's escape from slavery and her work on the Underground Railroad. It was published in 1869. The book was very popular, and Sarah shared the money she made from it with Harriet. This income helped pay Harriet's debts and saved her house.

A Helping Hero

In 1869, Harriet married Nelson Davis. He was a former slave who had joined the Union army. They were together for 18 years, until his death in 1888.

More than 30 years after the Civil War ended, the army began to give Harriet some of the money she deserved. She was given $20 each month, starting in 1897. But that wasn't for the work she did during the war. It was money the government owed to her husband, who had been a soldier.

Although Harriet didn't have much money, she always shared what she had with people who were less fortunate. Harriet took many people who were old, sick, and poor into her home. She cared for them, but her small home didn't have a lot of space.

Harriet cared about the health and happiness of others. She often took in elderly people and nursed them.

Harriet needed a larger building so she could help more people. In 1896, she used her small savings to buy 25 acres of land next to her house. There she helped create the Harriet Tubman Home for the Aged. The African Methodist Episcopal (AME) Zion Church ran the home, but Harriet worked there.

Harriet lived in her house until she became too old and sick to care for herself. Then she moved into the home for the aged next door so others could care for her. She died in 1913 from pneumonia, a lung disease.

Harriet Tubman received many honors before and after her death. In 1897, Queen Victoria of Great Britain awarded her a silver medal for bravery. The medal honored all that Harriet Tubman had done to help African-American slaves escape to the North and become free.

Although Harriet was not a Civil War soldier, she was buried with full military honors in Auburn, New York. The U.S. government did this to honor her for all of her important work during the Civil War as a spy, a scout, a cook, and a hospital nurse. To honor her further, the people in the town of Auburn set up a plaque in her memory.

Harriet Tubman changed—and probably saved—the

lives of hundreds of African Americans by leading them out of slavery to freedom. Her courage, bravery, and dedication inspired many people during her time. Her life continues to inspire people today.

This photo of Harriet was taken shortly before she died.

Harriet by the Numbers

5 Age at which she started her first job

19 Number of times she went south to lead slaves to freedom

29 Age at which she escaped slavery

300 Approximate number of slaves she led to freedom

800 Approximate number of slaves she helped free in Civil War raids

40,000 Number of dollars slave owners offered for her capture in the late 1850s

Harriet Tubman (far left) is shown with a group of slaves she helped escape to freedom.

Key Dates in the Life of Harriet Tubman

circa 1820 — Born near Bucktown, Maryland

Married John Tubman — **1844**

1849 — Used the Underground Railroad to escape from slavery

Made the first of 19 trips to the South to free slaves — **1850**

1861 Began four years of work for the Union army

1869 Married Nelson Davis

1896 Bought land in Auburn, New York, to build the Harriet Tubman Home for the Aged

1897 Received an honor from Britain's Queen Victoria for bravery

1913 Died in Auburn

Jackie Robinson

Strong Inside and Out

HERO *on the* FIELD

Jackie Robinson stepped onto the field in his new Brooklyn Dodgers baseball uniform. He was nervous. The crowd roared. Cameras flashed. Reporters scribbled on their notepads. It was 1947. Jack Roosevelt Robinson was the first African American to play baseball for a modern major-league team.

He was big news because he was breaking rules. Back in the 1940s, laws in many states told black people where they could live, work, and even eat. The sports world was also segregated. Baseball players who were African-American had to play

Left: Jackie Robinson in 1950
Above: A sign directs white citizens to a separate waiting area, which blacks weren't allowed to use, at a bus station in Jackson, Mississippi.

Jackie fields a ball.

in a league of their own, separate from white players.

Jackie Robinson was about to change all of that. When he walked onto Ebbets Field in Brooklyn, New York, on April 15, 1947, he knew he was ready to handle anything.

Branch Rickey, a co-owner of the Brooklyn Dodgers, had warned Jackie of what could happen. Some fans would be angry. Ballplayers might try to hurt him. Some teams might refuse to compete against a team with a black man. Jackie would have to hold his head up and play better than he ever had before.

Many people wondered if he could do it—if he could take the hard times and not fight back.

Jackie Robinson's answer to the world was yes!

CALIFORNIA, HERE WE COME

Jackie's mom, Mallie, had taught him to work hard in life and expect good things to happen. That was what Mallie taught all of her children. Jackie had three older brothers: Edgar, Frank, and Mack. Willa Mae, his only sister, was two years old when Jackie was born on January 31, 1919. His father, Jerry, left the family soon after. Jackie never saw him again.

The family lived on a farm in Cairo, Georgia. Jackie's grandparents, who had been slaves, lived nearby. When Jackie was sixteen months old, Mallie decided to move west. She'd heard there were better jobs for black people in California. So she packed up Jackie, his three brothers, and his sister. A few aunts, uncles, and cousins went, too. The close-knit family took the train from Georgia to Pasadena, California.

Jackie and his family pose for a portrait. From left are Mack, Jackie, Edgar, Mallie, Willa Mae, and Frank.

The Robinsons were one of the few black families in the city. At first, their white neighbors didn't like it when the Robinson kids played outside. Sometimes they called the police, even when the children hadn't done anything wrong! Mallie worked hard to stay friendly. Slowly, the neighbors got used to one another.

Jackie did well in elementary school. He liked to read and spent a lot of time at the library. But as he grew, he liked sports better than anything else. He also began to learn some hard lessons about his hometown. People with dark skin were treated differently than white people.

Pool Rules

Hispanics, African Americans, and Asians could use the town's public swimming pool and the local YMCA only one day a week. Jackie and his friends hated such an unfair rule. They decided to fight it the only way they could think of. They snuck into the reservoir that held the town's water and took a swim. That was against the law. Jackie and his friends called themselves the Pepper Street Gang. They got caught by the town sheriff. He took them to jail. Many people in Pasadena, including some of the police, thought Jackie might be starting a lifetime of being in trouble.

Tops in Sports

In high school, Jackie tried to be like his brothers. Two of them were natural athletes. His oldest brother, Edgar, was a speed skater. His brother Mack ran track at his college.

In 1936, when Jackie was still a teenager, Mack made the U.S. Olympic track team. He traveled across the world to Berlin, Germany, for the Olympic Games. At home in California, his family crowded around their radio to follow Mack's races.

As an adult, Jackie took his son, Jack, Jr., to visit his childhood home in Pasadena, California.

They cheered as they imagined what the races were like. They knew he had trained hard. His work paid off. He won a silver medal!

After that, Jackie began to run track, too. He was excellent at it, just as he was in the other sports he played—basketball, tennis, baseball, and football. But while Pasadena residents might have cheered for Jackie on his sports teams, the same people still didn't allow him to swim in the public pool.

Jackie wanted to go to college. He thought about attending the University of California, Los Angeles (UCLA). At the same time, he thought he should work and help his mother. He decided to start at a small college, Pasadena Junior College. It was closer to home, and it had a sports program. Mack had started there, too.

Two years later, Jackie changed colleges. He switched to UCLA. He became famous on campus, where he ran track and played football, baseball, and basketball. He ran so fast with the football that a newspaper nicknamed him Jackrabbit Jack.

At UCLA, he met a girl he liked very much—Rachel Isum, a nursing student. Jackie took classes in French, geometry, and physical education. He began to think about becoming a coach, or maybe even a professional athlete.

Then Jackie's brother Frank died after a motorcycle accident. Frank and Jackie had been very close. Jackie didn't talk much about how upset he was. He put his feelings into sports. He played harder than ever.

Jackie Quits

Jackie kept playing football for UCLA, but he lost hope

Jackie, like his brother Mack, was a broad jumper. Here, in 1939, Jackie takes part in an event at UCLA.

about his future in professional sports. In 1940, there were no black professional football, basketball, or baseball players. Jackie wasn't keeping his grades up. After four years, he was still in college. But the school rules would not allow him to play sports anymore. He didn't want to stay just to study. He wanted to play sports. His coaches and his girlfriend, Rachel, were against his quitting. They wanted him to work harder on his grades and graduate. Jackie decided to quit college to work full-time.

In 1941, Jackie found a job as a sports director at a youth camp in Northern California. He liked working with young people. At the camp, he set up games and sports programs. Jackie was starting a new life.

But half a world away, something else was starting—World War II.

Jackie's Values

When Jackie became an adult, he thought about how he wanted to live his life. He thought about how he wanted to be treated. And he thought about how he wanted to treat others. Here are nine guidelines he valued in life.

Citizenship: Do good works to help others improve their lives.

Commitment: If you make a promise to do something, be sure to keep your promise.

Courage: Do what you believe is the right thing—no matter how hard it may be.

Determination: Have a goal in mind and stick to it.

Excellence: Do your best at everything you try.

Integrity: Be true to your values and what you believe.

Justice: Be fair to all people.

Persistence: Don't give up on reaching your goals.

Teamwork: Work well with others and cooperate to reach a goal you all share.

JACKIE FIGHTS BACK

War changes people's lives everywhere. Jackie's world began to change in big ways. The camp closed and he lost his job. What did he know how to do, other than play football? Jackie heard about a spot on a semi-pro football team called the Honolulu Bears in Hawaii. He went for it and was hired.

When the team's season ended in early December 1941, Jackie sailed back to Los Angeles. His ship left Hawaii from the port of Pearl Harbor. Two days later, Japan bombed the naval base at Pearl Harbor. The United States entered World War II.

Young men were drafted, or called to serve, in the Army. Jackie's job hunt was over—at least for a few years. He became a soldier and went to basic training at Fort Riley, Kansas, in 1942. There he met Joe Louis,

Japanese planes bombed Pearl Harbor on December 7, 1941. The following day, the United States entered World War II.

the world heavyweight boxing champion. Joe was also doing basic training. Their friendship would last many years.

When basic training was done, Jackie was given the lowest rank in the military, private. He was assigned to a unit that cared for horses. He wanted a better job. He thought he could do more.

Black soldiers were allowed to serve only in all-black units. Jackie discovered that white men with the same education he had could go to officer training school. He could not.

Joe Louis decided to help Jackie. Joe asked a friend in Washington, D.C., to see what he could do. Soon after, Jackie and several other black soldiers were accepted to train to become officers in the Army.

Jackie (left) and Joe Louis first met in the Army. Their friendship lasted for years.

Officer Robinson

Jackie became an Army officer when he graduated from training school in 1943. He was now a second lieutenant. He wanted people at home to see how well he had done. So he went to Pasadena, wearing his sharp new uniform. Then he visited Rachel in Los Angeles. He asked her if she would marry him when he got out of the Army. Rachel said yes.

Jackie started his new Army job at Camp Hood, Texas. One day, he was riding the bus from town back to the base. He took a seat in the middle of the bus. The law in many parts of the country said that African Americans had to sit at the back, or stand up.

Jackie refused to move to the back. The bus driver reported him to the Camp Hood police. He said Jackie

Jackie proudly shows off his military uniform.

had used bad words and started a fight. Jackie was arrested. His case went to an Army trial. If he lost, he could be thrown out of the Army.

Luckily, some witnesses at the trial told the truth. Yes, he had sat in the middle of the bus, they said. But he had not hit anyone or started trouble. Jackie won his case. But the trial left him unhappy with the Army. So he wrote a letter asking to be let go. He was sent home in 1944.

Jackie went back to sports. Another soldier he'd met played with the Kansas City Monarchs baseball team. The Monarchs were one of the best-known teams in the Negro National League (one of several associations of African-American baseball players), and they were looking for players. Because Jackie had played baseball in school, he decided to try out for the team.

JACKIE BECOMES *a* STAR

The Negro National League was made up of famous teams such as the Homestead Grays and the Birmingham Black Barons. The Kansas City Monarchs were full of talent. They already had strong veteran players such as pitcher Leroy "Satchel" Paige.

Jackie hadn't played serious baseball since college. He knew he needed practice. He tried out anyway, hoping to get a spot. The Monarchs decided he was good enough to make the team. Jackie was hired to play shortstop.

The traveling life of the Negro leagues was hard for Jackie to get used to. Almost every night, the team was on the road, playing against a different team in a

In 1945, Jackie played shortstop for the Kansas City Monarchs.

different town. Some states had laws that kept African Americans and whites apart. This made the team's hard life even harder. Players couldn't enter most restaurants. Sometimes that meant sandwiches and sodas for breakfast. When they did have an extra day or two between games, they had to grab sleep on the bus—unless they found a hotel or rooming house that would accept African-American guests.

Jackie had been with the Monarchs only a short time when some scouts came to watch him play. He and other Negro leaguers often had been scouted by major-league teams. Nothing had happened. No team seemed ready for—or had players willing to accept—an African-American player.

Jackie didn't know it, but a man named Branch Rickey—co-owner of the Brooklyn Dodgers, a team in the National League—had made up his mind to do an experiment.

Branch knew that there were fine players in the Negro leagues who could help the Dodgers win a World Series championship. He knew it would be difficult. Some other owners might try to stop him. So he pretended he was starting another all-black team, which he called the Brooklyn Brown Dodgers. He wanted his plan to remain a secret until he found just the right man.

It was Rickey's scouts who had seen Jackie in 1945. They returned to New York with good reports. Rickey invited Jackie to a meeting.

Jackie found out what Branch Rickey was up to when he arrived. Jackie remembered it this way:

> When I walked into Mr. Rickey's office, he was puffing on a big cigar. He rose from his leather swivel chair and shook my hand.
>
> Mr. Rickey got right to the point. "I think you can play in the major leagues," he said.
>
> I was batting over .300, and I had stolen a lot of bases. But there were plenty of older, more established Negro league stars. Why me?
>
> Mr. Rickey had been looking for a black player who could stand up to taunts from bullies and racists. He thought I was that man.
>
> Mr. Rickey warned that I would face beanballs [pitches that hit the batter] and fists. He said I would be called dirty names. He told me I'd have to permit all those things to happen and not lose my temper.

"Mr. Rickey," I asked, "are you looking for a Negro who is afraid to fight back?"

"Robinson," he rumbled, "I'm looking for a ballplayer with guts enough not to fight back."

There were no Brown Dodgers at all, Rickey admitted. Did Jackie want a chance to become a Brooklyn Dodger? Of course! Was he willing to first play for the Montreal Royals, the Dodgers' "farm," or training, team in Canada? Jackie was willing.

Then Rickey went on. What would Jackie do if a white player spat on him? What if white fans booed him or threw things? What if a pitcher tried to hit him with a beanball? All of these things might happen, because many people in 1945 didn't like the idea of whites and blacks playing together on the same team.

Jackie sat up straighter. Rickey didn't know anything

"It Ain't Bragging!"

Leroy "Satchel" Paige was never short on words or slow with a baseball. He spent most of his career in the Negro leagues and was one of the greatest pitchers in history.

Satchel was a country boy from Alabama who

about him. He was strong. He was tough. Jackie Robinson could fight back!

But was he tough enough *not* to fight back? Could Jackie be above the people who called him names because of his race? Could he ignore people who threw things at him?

Jackie thought about it. He thought of his mother and also his grandmother, who had survived slavery.

Jackie, in his Montreal Royals uniform, gets ready to wow the fans.

They had always reminded him to be proud of being black. They had told him that what mattered most was

became a baseball star with his amazing skills. He loved showing off from the mound. He called his pitches bloopers, loopers, wobbly balls, and nothin' balls.

By the time Jackie Robinson broke the color barrier in the major leagues, Satchel was 42 years old. The Cleveland Indians hired him to play in 1948 as the oldest rookie in major-league history. Satchel threw a shutout in a game against the Chicago White Sox and helped the Indians win the American League pennant. Satchel was voted into the Baseball Hall of Fame in 1971. "If you can do it," he said, "it ain't bragging!"

not what people said about him. What mattered most was trying to be a good person on the inside. Jackie began to understand what was expected of him.

Meeting the Challenge

Jackie knew that if he agreed, he had to show that he was as strong on the inside as he was on the outside. Jackie could prove to the world that the kind of man he was had nothing to do with the color of his skin. He could also do two things he had wanted to do for a long time. He could marry Rachel and play professional ball. Jackie believed he could meet the challenge.

He signed a contract with Rickey to play for the Montreal Royals.

If Jackie did well with the Royals, he would move up to the Dodgers—a major-league team in the National League.

Jackie and Rachel get married. Their good friend Karl Downs performed the ceremony.

STRONG INSIDE *and* OUT

Spring training was in Daytona, Florida. Traveling through the South to get there was a challenge for Jackie and Rachel. Because the Robinsons were African-American, the airline asked them to give up their seats on one leg of their trip. When they finally got on another airplane, the same thing happened again.

Finally, an angry Jackie and Rachel took a bus and rode for hours. They sat in the back.

Once they reached Florida, they didn't have a room in the same hotel as the rest of the team. The South's Jim Crow laws forbade black and white people from staying in the same hotels. Already, Jackie was being treated differently than the other players.

Jackie couldn't wait to put all this behind him and start training. As weeks passed, he sharpened his batting skills and began to fit in with the rest of the team. Rachel came to watch him practice every day. In the Royals' season opener, Jackie hit a home run. His teammates saw that he could help them win. Things were going well.

Wherever the Royals went to play, there was trouble. One team said they would not show up for a game if the Royals brought Jackie. In another town, a mob of angry white people came to the field before the game, looking

for Jackie. He and Rachel had to leave town—fast.

At some stadiums, angry white fans shouted ugly words and called Jackie awful names. Jackie held his anger inside, but he had trouble sleeping. Sometimes he couldn't eat. When he found out that Rachel was going to have a baby, he also worried about her health.

But somehow, when Jackie played ball, he focused on the game and his playing. He put all other thoughts out of his head.

The Royals had a winning season and headed for the Junior World Series against the Louisville

Living with Jim Crow

From the 1880s until the early 1960s, many states had laws keeping black and white people separate from one another. The name of the laws came from a white actor who dressed as a black character called Jim Crow. Here are just a few:

Jim Crow Laws

North Carolina "The commission is empowered . . . to require the establishment of separate waiting rooms at all [train and bus] stations for the white and colored races."

Alabama "It shall be unlawful to conduct a restaurant . . . at which white and colored people are served in the same room."

Georgia "It shall be unlawful for colored people to frequent any park owned . . . by the city for the benefit, use, and enjoyment of white persons."

Missouri "It shall be unlawful for any colored child to attend any white school, or any white child to attend a colored school."

Jackie is congratulated by a teammate after hitting a home run at his first Montreal game, on April 18, 1946.

Colonels. The first games of the series—the minor leagues' version of the World Series—were in Kentucky.

It would have been very difficult for Louisville to back out of the series or refuse to play. They agreed to allow Jackie on the field—but they closed part of the black seating section of the stadium so that most black fans couldn't get into the games. An African-American player could play—but black fans wouldn't be able to enjoy seeing him.

The Louisville fans were the worst Jackie had ever seen. He went into a batting slump. From time to time during their careers, many players have trouble hitting. For Jackie, the timing was horrible. Having lost in Louisville, the Royals went back to Montreal to play the next games.

Cheers for Jackie

It helped that the fans in Montreal loved Jackie. No matter how badly the visiting team or its fans acted toward him, the Royals fans would cheer for Jackie. The Royals took the lead. Jackie scored the last, winning run.

Jackie was the first Royal to win the league batting crown. His season batting average was .349. He'd scored 113 runs and stolen 40 bases.

Jackie had survived his first Royals season as a hero, but he had other things on his mind. He and Rachel were about to become parents. Jack, Jr., was born in California in November 1946. Jackie spent the holidays with his new family.

He still had a Royals contract. He planned to play basketball during the off-season and then report to spring training in March. Still, he and everyone else in baseball were wondering if and when Branch Rickey would take his experiment to the big leagues.

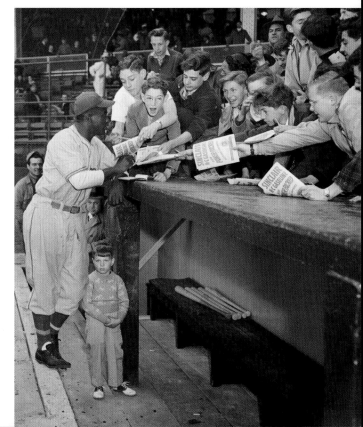

Jackie signs autographs for Montreal Royals fans while a batboy patiently waits.

WELCOME
to the
BIG LEAGUES

Before the start of the 1947 season, the Royals went to Brooklyn, New York, to play exhibition games—games that didn't affect the team's standing in the league.

Everyone was talking about Jackie Robinson. Jackie knew just when to bunt and when to slam the ball into the outfield. He seemed to have fun as he snuck past a baseman for a steal. Other players began to admire his skills.

The Big Day

On April 10, Jackie went to Ebbets Field, the home stadium of the Dodgers. The Dodgers had bought Jackie's contract from the Royals. He had made it! He was the first African-American player in the major leagues.

On opening day, April 15, 1947, Jackie Robinson covered first base. Rachel and Jack, Jr., had just flown in from California. His hard work had paid off. Jackie was in the big leagues. He had broken the color barrier.

Jackie, still in his Royals uniform, enters the Dodgers' locker room. He came out of the changing room as a Dodger.

Jackie's early days as a Dodger were not easy. A few of the Dodgers had come from the South and kept their southern ideas about race. They didn't want to play with Jackie. They asked Branch Rickey to fire him. Of course, Rickey refused.

Jackie Remembers

This is Jackie's memory of those first few games:

> At first, I was very nervous. But gradually I began to relax and play my game. Sadly, Mr. Rickey's predictions all came true. I was called names by fans and other players—and even by some of my teammates.

There were insults. There were balls pitched at my head. There were players who deliberately cut me with their spikes. There were death threats. At times, I felt deeply sorry for myself. At times, I wondered if being the first Negro in the majors was worth it.

And at times I wanted to fight back. But I had promised Mr. Rickey that I wouldn't.

The New York fans welcomed Jackie and his exciting way of playing. He kept the pitchers on their toes. And the way he stole bases drove the crowd wild! When the Dodgers went on the road, Jackie was cheered by most black fans and booed by most white fans. Hate letters came in the mail to the Robinsons' home. Jackie had to remind himself again and again to keep his cool.

In Philadelphia, the manager of the Phillies led his team in nasty name-calling when Jackie came onto the field. Fans of all races wrote to the league commissioner to complain. It was in Philadelphia that the Dodgers began to stand as a team behind Jackie. They respected him for doing his job even when things around him were hard.

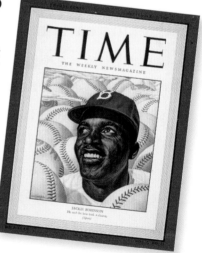

Jackie was on the cover of the September 22, 1947, issue of TIME magazine. The words under his picture say, "He and the boss took a chance."

Jackie was famous for sliding into home plate.

Henry "Hank" Aaron, a famed African-American baseball player who started playing in the major leagues in 1954, wrote about Jackie's early days on the field: "To this day, I don't know how he withstood the things he did without lashing back. I've been through a lot in my time, and I consider myself to be a patient man, but I know I couldn't have done what Jackie did. I don't think anybody else could have done it. Somehow, though, Jackie had the strength to suppress his instincts, to sacrifice his pride for his people's. It was an incredible act of selflessness that brought the races closer together than ever before and shaped the dreams of an entire generation."

The 1947 Dodgers became league champions. Jackie won the Rookie of the Year Award. The Brooklyn fans were so proud that they held a Jackie Robinson Day.

Jackie and Rachel get the keys to their new Cadillac.

Jackie's and Rachel's mothers came to help celebrate. Jackie received many special gifts, including a fancy gold watch and a brand-new Cadillac, one of the finest cars of the time.

But the greatest gift was perhaps that the Brooklyn Dodgers had fully accepted Jackie Robinson as a key member of the team.

Baseball's Origins

Variations of baseball have been played since the late 1700s. The version closest to what we have today can be traced back to the Knickerbocker Base Ball Club of New York, which came up with a list of rules for the game in 1845.

Here are some early rules of baseball:

- Pitches are to be thrown underhand.

- A ball caught on the first bounce is an out.

- A ball hit out of the field is a foul.

PAVING
the WAY

A fter Jackie, more and more black players joined Major League Baseball. Larry Doby became the first in the American League, not long after Jackie. He played for the Cleveland Indians. Roy Campanella and Don Newcombe joined the Dodgers. Jackie Robinson had paved the way.

By 1962, several Negro league players had joined National League teams. These players got together before a spring training game between the Brooklyn Dodgers and the Boston Braves. From left are Jackie Robinson, George Crowe, Joe Black, Sam Jethroe, Roy Campanella, and Bill Bruton.

Sports Firsts

Jackie Robinson once said: "My breakthrough . . . paved the way for many fine athletes to come after me." Here are some African-American sports firsts.

Basketball: Earl Lloyd of the Washington Capitals was the first African American to play in an NBA game, on October 31, 1950.

Tennis: Althea Gibson was the first African American to play in the U.S. Open and the first African-American winner, in 1957.

Ice Hockey: Willie O'Ree was the first African American to play professional ice hockey. He joined the Boston Bruins in 1958.

Gymnastics: Dominique Dawes was the first African American to win an individual medal (bronze) in gymnastics at the Olympic Games, in 1996.

In the 1950s, doors were opening all over America. Jackie Robinson had given many African Americans the courage to fight for equal rights. He had stopped accepting unfairness in silence. Jackie began to speak out more and more. He published a book about his life, *Jackie Robinson: My Own Story*. A movie was made from it in 1950. Jackie played himself!

Jackie's major-league career lasted almost ten years, all of them with the Dodgers. The team won six league pennants and a World Series championship title. The 1956 season was his last. The Dodgers were moving to California.

Jackie ends his ten-year career with a wave.

Jackie found out they were planning to trade him to the New York Giants. But he was already thinking of leaving baseball.

He wasn't as fast as he used to be. He wasn't playing as well as he wished. And by then he and Rachel were the parents of Jack, Jr., Sharon, and David. He wanted time with his family.

Jackie announced that he would retire. He was ready to live a life outside baseball.

New Careers

Jackie worked in business as a vice president at Chock full o'Nuts, a coffee company. He wrote a newspaper column. He helped start a bank. Jackie met U.S. presidents and movie stars. He traveled and went deep-sea fishing with his family.

In 1962, he was elected to the National Baseball Hall of Fame. The ceremony was held in Cooperstown, New York. It was one of the proudest days of his life. Two important people from his early years were there to celebrate: his mother, Mallie, and Branch Rickey.

Jackie's concern with opening doors kept him busy. His whole family took part in the 1963 March on Washington for equal rights for African Americans. The Robinsons stood with tens of thousands of Americans of all races to hear Dr. Martin Luther King, Jr., give his famous "I Have a Dream" speech.

In 1957, Jackie Robinson (left) and Dr. Martin Luther King, Jr., received honorary degrees from Howard University.

Jackie believed in King's words about different races working and living together. That was what his baseball career had been all about. He worked to bring more black managers and coaches to baseball. And he and Rachel raised money to help fight for civil rights. To do this, they started

Jackie tried hard to get companies to hire African Americans.

having "Afternoon of Jazz" concerts each summer in their big backyard in Stamford, Connecticut. As the children grew up, they helped plan some of the concerts.

In 1971, tragedy struck. Jack, Jr., was killed in a car accident on his way home from work. Jackie and Rachel pulled together to handle this terrible tragedy.

The family continued to work and give back. Jackie started a company to build homes for people who didn't have much money.

Then, in 1972, Jackie died suddenly of a heart attack. Tens of thousands of people lined the streets of New York City to watch his funeral and to say goodbye. Jackie would be missed. His pride in being black would always be admired. His courage and strength—on and off the baseball field—would never be forgotten.

In 1997, 50 years after Jackie Robinson walked out onto Ebbets Field, baseball honored him. Bill Clinton,

Thousands of people watched as Jackie's funeral took place. After the service, Rachel Robinson (center) is helped into a car by her son David (left) and the Reverend Jesse Jackson (right).

President Bill Clinton applauds Rachel Robinson during ceremonies at Shea Stadium on April 15, 1997.

then president of the United States, came to New York to the Mets' Shea Stadium. Baseball Commissioner Bud Selig was there. Rachel and Sharon were there, too.

Jackie Robinson has been honored on three different U.S. Postal Service stamps. This one is from 1999.

They came together to show that what Jackie accomplished was about more than baseball. It was about making a better world. Jackie's uniform number, 42, was retired forever. Bud Selig said that number 42 belonged to Jackie Robinson "for the ages."

In 2003, the U.S. Congress voted to give Jackie the Congressional Gold Medal. It's one of the nation's highest honors.

Baseball cards commemorate Jackie's time with the Brooklyn Dodgers.

Many people still face closed doors. But Jackie Robinson endured much and fought hard to open them. He was strong inside and out. That's why he will always be a special man— "for the ages."

Key Dates in the Life of Jackie Robinson

1919 — Born on January 31, in Cairo, Georgia

Enrolled at UCLA; starred in football and track — **1939**

1942 — Enlisted in the U.S. Army

Signed with the Kansas City Monarchs of the Negro leagues; later signed with the Brooklyn Dodgers' minor-league team in Montreal, Canada — **1945**

1947 — Began playing for the Dodgers

Won the National League's Most Valuable Player Award — 1949

1957 — Retired from baseball

1962 — Voted into the Baseball Hall of Fame

Died on October 24, in Stamford, Connecticut — 1972

#42 fully retired after Mariano Rivera (who was already wearing #42 when Jackie's number was first retired) played his last game — 2013

Rosa Parks

Civil Rights Pioneer

TIRED *of* GIVING IN

On December 1, 1955, Rosa Parks stepped onto a bus—and into history.

For Rosa, that Thursday began like any other day. She went to work at a department store in Montgomery, Alabama. Rosa was a seamstress there. She fitted clothes for customers. Sometimes white customers were rude to her. Because Rosa was black, they did not see her as an equal. But Rosa couldn't defend herself, or she might get in trouble. So she stayed calm, kept quiet, and did her job.

After work, Rosa boarded a city bus to go home. As always, she walked past the first five rows. These rows were empty, but they were marked "Whites Only."

Rosa Parks in 1956

In the 1950s, only white people were allowed to sit in the front seats of trolleys and buses in the South.

It was against the law for black people to sit there. At that time, Alabama and other southern states had laws that were unfair to black citizens. These segregation laws said that black people had to drink from separate water fountains, go to separate schools, and ride in a separate part of the bus.

Rosa found a seat in the first row of the "Colored" section. Black passengers were allowed to sit there— unless white riders needed the seats.

As the bus continued on its route, all the seats filled up. The driver noticed that a white man was standing. The driver looked at Rosa and the other black passengers.

"I want those seats," the driver said.

At first, no one moved. Then the man sitting beside Rosa moved to the back. The city's laws said that a black person could not sit in the same row as a white person. Rosa would have to move so that the white man could sit. But Rosa did not budge.

She was tired of giving in to unfair laws. And she was tired of being mistreated. Rosa had to stick up for herself.

"Are you going to stand up?" asked the driver.

"No," Rosa answered quietly.

"Well, I'm going to have you arrested," he warned.

Rosa looked the driver in the eye. "You may do that."

Soon, two white police officers arrived. One of them asked Rosa why she hadn't given up her seat.

She asked him a question in return. "Why do you all push us around?"

"The law's the law, and you're under arrest," he answered.

Rosa hated segregation, and she hoped that the laws would change one day. She could not have known what her act of courage would start.

Rosa refused to give up her seat on a bus much like this one from the 1950s.

LIFE *on the* FARM

Rosa was born on February 4, 1913, in Tuskegee, Alabama. Her parents were Leona and James McCauley. Leona was a teacher before Rosa was born. James was a carpenter.

Life was not easy for Rosa and her family. Her father often worked far away from home. He was gone for months at a time. Leona stayed at home with Rosa. She missed her husband. She wished that he would get a job close to home. But Rosa's father liked building houses and refused to quit. He and his wife often argued about his decision.

When Rosa was 2, she and her parents moved in with her grandparents, Sylvester and Rose. They lived on a farm in the small town of Pine Level, Alabama. It was where Rosa's mother had grown up. Rosa's family was proud of the little farm. They were not rich, but they were the only black family that owned land in Pine Level.

Some black people in the South owned farms like this. Rosa's grandparents had a small farm in Alabama.

Rosa soon had a baby brother named Sylvester. Rosa's parents continued to argue. Her father left the family and moved to another city. When Rosa was 5 years old, he came for a short visit. After that, Rosa did not see her father again until she was an adult.

A Close Family

To help support her family, Rosa's mother worked at a school that was eight miles from home. It was the closest teaching job she could find. The family did not own a car, so Rosa's mother stayed near school during the week. On weekends, she came back to Pine Level and cared for her children. She took her kids to church and taught them at home. Rosa learned to read when she was only 4 years old.

Rosa missed her mother, but she loved living with her grandparents. She went fishing with them and helped on the farm. She collected eggs from the chickens and picked fruit and pecans from the trees. Rosa helped her grandparents in other ways, too. Sometimes Rosa worked on a neighbor's farm. She earned $1 for every 100 pounds of cotton she picked. It was hard work, but it helped support the family.

When she was not working on the farm, Rosa enjoyed listening to her grandparents' stories. Both of them had a lot to teach Rosa.

In the South, entire families often worked in the cotton fields.

Grandfather Sylvester had been born a slave. When he was a boy, he was beaten by his owners. Sylvester never forgot the way he had been treated. He taught Rosa never to accept bad treatment from anyone.

Teaching Honesty

Grandma Rose also had been a slave. She told Rosa not to judge people. She taught her to be honest and respectful. Rosa usually did as she was told.

Rosa started school when she was 6. The law said that blacks and whites had to go to separate schools.

The school for white students was big and new. It had a lot of teachers. Rosa and the other black children in Pine Level went to a tiny one-room schoolhouse. There was one teacher for 50 students. Rosa liked learning and earned good grades. But she did not understand why black people and white people were not treated equally.

Troubled Nights

The Ku Klux Klan (KKK) is a hate group that has used violence and terror to achieve its goals. Its members believe in white supremacy. They aim to restrict the rights of anyone not like their members, including blacks, Jews, and immigrants. The KKK is not as active as it once was, but some people still belong to it.

The KKK was formed after the Civil War. Klansmen burned homes and even murdered people. When Rosa Parks was a girl, the KKK was more active than it is today. At night, Rosa's grandfather would sit on the front porch holding a shotgun. He felt he needed to protect his family. Sometimes Rosa sat with him. She understood what it was like to fear people who were filled with hate. She learned the importance of standing up for one's rights.

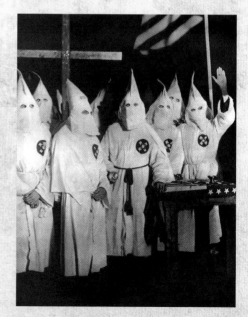

Members of the Ku Klux Klan often wear hoods to hide their identities.

SEPARATE
and UNEQUAL

When Rosa was 11, her school in Pine Level closed. But Rosa's mother cared about her daughter's education. She took a second job as a maid and saved her money. Then she sent Rosa to a private school for black girls.

The school's name was the Montgomery Industrial School, but all the students called it Miss White's school. Miss Alice White was one of the founders and the principal. She was a white woman from the North who wanted to teach in the South. She believed that all Americans should have a good education.

Miss White's school was in Montgomery, the capital of Alabama. The city is 25 miles from Pine Level. Rosa had an aunt and cousins in Montgomery. She stayed with them while she went to school.

Rosa studied English, science, and other subjects. She took classes in cooking and sewing, too. Sewing was one of Rosa's favorite activities. She liked making her own dresses and aprons.

Outside of school, Rosa learned hard lessons about segregation. She knew a little about segregation already. In Pine Level, black people and white people went to different schools and churches. But the town was too small to have segregated buses or trains. In Montgomery, almost everything was segregated. Blacks and whites had separate libraries, bathrooms, lunch counters, and phone booths.

Why did Alabama and other states get away with treating black people unfairly? One reason was the U.S. government. In 1896, the U.S. Supreme Court ruled in favor of segregation in a case called *Plessy v. Ferguson*. Homer Plessy was a black man who had been arrested for sitting in the part of a train that was reserved for whites only.

Rosa left Pine Level for Alabama's state capital, Montgomery, when she was 11.

The court said that a state could make black people sit in separate train cars from white people if the services in the cars were equal. This was known

Most schools for black children (like this one) were overcrowded and lacked supplies.

as the "separate but equal" rule. Alabama and other states used the rule to allow segregation in public places. But forcing one part of the population to use separate facilities puts them at a disadvantage. Separate can never really be equal.

Because of segregation, black people had to drink from different water fountains, go through different entrances at movie theaters and other public places, and eat in different restaurants.

Changes Ahead

In 1928, when Rosa was in 9th grade, Miss White's school closed. Rosa stayed in Montgomery and went to a public junior high school for black students. Then she went to the only black high school around. It was run by the

Alabama State Teachers College. Rosa dreamed of becoming a nurse or teacher.

But when Rosa was in 11th grade, her grandma Rose got sick. Rosa went home to care for her. Grandma Rose soon died. Then Rosa's mother became ill, too. Rosa stayed home and nursed her mother back to health. Sadly, Rosa had to quit school. "It was just something that had to be done," she said later.

The Harlem Renaissance

For many Americans, the 1920s brought big changes to the country. Fashion changed, with girls wearing short skirts and bright lipstick. Many families owned automobiles for the first time, and the first movies with sound were made.

Zora Neale Hurston wrote several novels drawing on her experience as an African American.

Many blacks artists, writers, and musicians moved to Harlem, in New York City. Artists William Johnson and Jacob Lawrence, writers Zora Neale Hurston and Langston Hughes, singer Ethel Waters, and composer William Grant Still all lived in Harlem during this time.

This period became known as the Harlem Renaissance. African Americans produced powerful art, music, and literature, and established a sense of cultural identity and pride.

ROSA GROWS UP

When Rosa was 18, she met someone who would change her life. Raymond Parks, whom everyone called Parks, was ten years older than Rosa. He worked as a barber. Barbershops were important gathering spots for black men. They would discuss politics and civil rights—the equal treatment of all people under the law. Parks had many friends and always knew what was happening in the city.

Parks fell in love with Rosa right away. He asked her to marry him on their second date. But Rosa wanted to get to know him better. She soon discovered that Parks was one of the smartest people she had ever met. Parks was fun, too. He took Rosa for rides in his red sports car. Rosa married Parks two years later, in 1932.

Working Together

Parks helped Rosa achieve her dreams. He encouraged her to go back to high school. Rosa earned her diploma when she was 20.

Parks also talked to Rosa about the National Association for the Advancement of Colored People. It was called the NAACP for short. Parks was active in the organization. He was helping the NAACP fight for black people's civil rights.

Rosa was curious about the NAACP. One night in 1943, she went to a meeting in Montgomery. The members welcomed Rosa and asked her to be the group's secretary. Rosa agreed. Now she had two jobs. During the day, she worked as a secretary on an Army base. At night, she volunteered with the NAACP. She answered mail, organized meetings, and took notes. She also did work for E.D. Nixon, a local leader of the

This is an NAACP office in Detroit, Michigan. Raymond Parks was active in the civil rights group.

NAACP. The mistreatment of black citizens had always bothered Rosa. Now she was doing something about it.

One issue that was especially important to Rosa was voting. She knew that voting meant power. If people voiced their opinions through their votes, politicians would have to listen to them. Then life for black people could improve. Rosa joined the Montgomery Voters League. She and many other volunteers worked hard to help black people register, or sign up, to vote.

This was no easy job. Although black people had the right to vote in Alabama, rules often kept them from registering. For example, black voters were allowed to register to vote only on certain days and at certain hours—usually in the middle of the workday. Also, black citizens had to take a test before they could register.

These voting rules were unfair. They seemed especially unfair to black war veterans and soldiers. Rosa's brother, Sylvester, had fought in World War II. He had risked his life for his country. But when he returned to the United States, he was not even allowed to vote.

Rosa was angry. She firmly believed that everyone should be allowed to vote, as guaranteed by the 15th Amendment to the Constitution. And she was determined to help make that happen. Even though the KKK often killed people who helped blacks register,

Tough Tests

States that wanted to prevent black citizens from voting often required them to take a "literacy" test. If people wanted to vote, they had to pass the test—but only if they did not own land. Since many whites owned land, they didn't have to take the test.

The exam questions were difficult, and the test takers were not always told which ones they got wrong. The people giving the test could also choose which questions to ask. Rosa was educated, and it still took her three tries before she passed the test!

To make voting even more difficult, blacks were often asked questions that were impossible to answer, such as: How many bubbles are in a bar of soap? How many seeds are in a watermelon? How many hairs are on a hog's back? How high is up?

Today, all U.S. citizens over the age of 18 are allowed to vote. They do not have to own land. And they do not have to take a test.

Rosa didn't let her fear stop her from volunteering.

Over time, Rosa found another way to help, too. She advised the NAACP Youth Council. The council was made up of black teens. She taught the teens to believe in themselves and to fight for their rights.

Battle on the Bus

One day in 1943, Rosa had an awful experience on a bus. She entered through the front door and paid her 10 cents. The driver ordered Rosa to get off the bus

Members of the **NAACP** Youth Council met to socialize and fight for equal rights.

and then get on again—this time using the back door. His order was legal. Drivers often enforced the law. Sometimes they drove away while black passengers walked to the back door.

Rosa saw that it was very crowded near the back, so she stayed where she was. The driver walked over to her, grabbed her sleeve, and pushed her toward the door. Proud and angry, Rosa got off the bus and did not get back on. She didn't know the driver's name, but she'd remember his face. She would see him again 12 years later.

MAKING HISTORY

As the years passed, Rosa stayed busy. She got a job as a seamstress at the Montgomery Fair department store. She also did sewing work for a white couple, Virginia and Clifford Durr. Like Rosa, they believed that blacks should have the same rights as whites. Rosa and the couple became good friends.

An excellent seamstress, Rosa earned her living altering clothes.

Rosa also continued working with the NAACP and fighting for the rights of black people. In 1954, an important court case caught her attention. It was called *Brown v. Board of Education*. In this famous case, a black couple in Topeka, Kansas, was angry that their daughter Linda Brown couldn't go to the school for white children near their house. After a long court battle, the U.S. Supreme Court ruled that states could no

Linda Brown (in front row), whose father started an important court case

longer have separate schools for white people and black people. Rosa was thrilled. If the court stopped segregation in schools, maybe it would stop segregation on buses, too. Rosa hoped these other changes would come soon.

One year after the Supreme Court ruling, Rosa was invited to a ten-day workshop in Tennessee. The Highlander Folk School was run by people who trained others to work for social justice. They wanted to make sure that schools were integrated. Both black and white people attended the workshop. They ate together and

Students at the Highlander Folk School, including Rosa (center), take a break.

talked together about ways to bring about change. This was the first place Rosa had ever been where black and white people were considered equals. She learned how to help people work for civil rights. She felt happy and hopeful.

Then Rosa went back to Montgomery and its unfair laws. This was very hard for her. She went back to riding segregated buses.

Rosa's Arrest

On December 1, 1955, Rosa left work to go home after a hard day. She got on the Cleveland Avenue bus, deposited her fare, and took a seat. At first, she did not notice who was driving. Then she recognized the driver's face. He was the same man who had thrown her off the bus 12 years earlier. His name was James Blake.

The next few moments would change history. The bus filled, and the driver ordered Rosa to give up her seat to a white man. Rosa refused. She sat quietly while the driver called the police. When the officers arrived,

After Rosa's arrest, a police officer takes her fingerprints.

they arrested Rosa and drove her to the police station.
They took her photograph and fingerprints. Then they
put her in a jail cell.

Two hours later, Rosa was allowed to call home.
Clifford and Virginia Durr, E.D. Nixon, and her
husband, Parks, all came. The bail to get her out of jail
was $100, which was a lot of money then. Rosa's
friends paid the money and brought her home.

Rosa would have to go to court on Monday,
December 5. The court would decide if Rosa was
guilty of breaking the segregation laws.

A Big Plan

That night, Rosa and her friends stayed up late talking. E.D.
suggested that they should try to take Rosa's case to the U.S.

Supreme Court. He and the NAACP would prove that the bus laws went against the Constitution—the highest law in the United States. The Constitution says that everyone must be treated equally. If the Supreme Court decided that the bus laws went against the Constitution, the laws would have to change. This was what had happened with *Brown v. Board of Education*, and it could happen again.

E.D. thought that Rosa was the perfect person to challenge the bus laws in court. She was dignified and polite. And she wasn't afraid to speak up for herself.

But Rosa was not so sure about the plan. She did not like being in the spotlight. Her husband was worried, too. But finally Rosa agreed.

E.D. immediately began calling black leaders in the community to tell them about the plan. Soon, the news reached a black professor named Jo Ann Robinson. She headed a group called the Women's Political Council. Robinson suggested that black leaders should start a boycott. They should encourage black people to stay off the city buses on Monday, the day of Rosa's trial. The boycott would do three things. It would hurt the bus company. (About three-fourths of the city's bus riders were black. If they did not ride the buses, the company would lose money.) It would show support for Rosa. And it would show that black people were firm that segregation had to end.

THE BUS
BOYCOTT

The Women's Political Council printed 35,000 flyers to tell people about the boycott. The flyers said: "Don't ride the bus to work, to town, to school, or anywhere, on Monday, December 5. If you work, take a cab or walk."

The next morning, council members distributed the flyers at schools and stores. Meanwhile, E.D. Nixon called the newspaper and the city's black leaders to help spread the word. By Friday evening, most people knew about the plan.

But Rosa's boycott had already begun. She had decided that she would never set foot on a segregated bus again. She took a cab instead of a bus to work that day. At lunchtime, she met with Fred Gray. He was the black lawyer hired by the NAACP to represent her.

Residents of Montgomery, Alabama, walked to work for months during the bus boycott.

That weekend, she met with leaders at the Dexter Avenue Baptist Church to go over the boycott plans. Everyone was ready.

On Monday, December 5, Rosa went to court. She was found guilty, and was ordered to pay a $14 fine. After the trial, Gray spoke to reporters. He said that the city's bus laws were unjust and that he would ask the U.S. Supreme Court to review Rosa's case. He also said that Rosa would not pay the fine.

Outside, the boycott went on as planned. Blacks stayed off the buses. They walked or shared rides. Black cab owners helped out. They gave people rides for 10 cents—the same price as a bus fare. Children ran behind some of the buses, shouting, "No riders today!" They were right. Montgomery's buses were nearly empty. The boycott was a success.

On Monday night, the black leaders met at the Holt Street Baptist Church to review how the boycott had gone. This time, nearly 5,000 people arrived to show their support. They spilled out of the church and onto the sidewalk. Rosa attended the meeting and sat right up front with the boycott's leaders. When a minister introduced her, the crowd chanted her name and shouted their thanks.

Almost everyone agreed that the boycott had worked. They decided to continue it until the bus laws changed. The black leaders had chosen a young Baptist minister to take charge of the boycott. His name was Dr. Martin Luther King, Jr., Rosa admired the young preacher. The two of them became friends.

Dr. King gave a speech that night. "We are here this evening to say to those who have mistreated us so long that we are tired—tired of being segregated and humiliated," he said. The crowd stood and cheered.

Dr. Martin Luther King, Jr., encourages the boycotters.

The Boycott Gathers Support

The boycott was not easy. As weeks stretched into months, people had to find new ways to get to work and school. Some of them formed carpools. Some rode bikes. But most of them walked. They walked until their feet were sore. They walked until they wore out their shoes. People from all over the country heard about the boycott. Many of them sent shoes and money to show their support.

The protest was especially hard for Rosa. She began to get phone calls from some angry white people. Some even threatened to kill her. Rosa and her husband both lost their jobs. Rosa was even arrested again, this time for boycotting. Montgomery city officials had found an old law that said boycotting was illegal. They also arrested hundreds of other boycotters. Still, Rosa's strength—and her belief that she was doing the right thing—kept her going.

Sweet Success

People could see that the boycott was working. The bus company was losing money. So were some stores in town. Because black people had stopped riding buses, they did not go downtown to shop. Business owners were getting worried.

Dr. Martin Luther King, Jr., and other boycott leaders wait to hear the Supreme Court's decision. The department store where Rosa worked is in the background.

Six months after the boycott began, the U.S. Supreme Court agreed to review Rosa's case. Now the whole country waited to hear what the court would decide. Would it say that bus segregation was fair? Or would it vote to stop the laws?

On November 13, 1956, the court made its decision. It ruled that segregation on city buses in Alabama was unconstitutional. Montgomery would have to stop separating blacks and whites on its buses. A few weeks later, on December 20, the U.S. Supreme Court delivered its order in writing. After 381 days, black people once again boarded Montgomery's buses. But now they could sit wherever they chose.

OUT *of the* SPOTLIGHT

I n December 1956, Rosa boarded a Montgomery city bus for the first time in more than a year. She sat in the front row. She was happy that no one could ever force her to move again. "When I declined to give up my seat, it was not that day, or bus, in particular," Rosa said years later. "I just wanted to be free, like everybody else."

Rosa was proud that she had helped bring about important change—not just in Montgomery, but all over the South. Black people in other cities saw what had happened in Montgomery. They began their own boycotts, marches, and protests. The civil rights movement was in full swing.

For a while, Rosa and her husband continued to live in Montgomery. Rosa kept working with the NAACP.

She traveled to schools and churches all over the United States, speaking about her arrest and about civil rights. Still jobless, Rosa and Parks struggled to get by.

A Move North

By 1957, Rosa was ready for a change. She was still getting threats from people who were angry about her activist work, and she was tired of living in fear. Along with her husband and mother, she moved to Detroit, Michigan. Rosa's brother, Sylvester, had settled there years before.

In Detroit, Rosa joined the local chapter of the NAACP. She continued to give speeches about her experiences. One day, a college president heard Rosa speak. He offered her a job at the Hampton Institute in Virginia. Rosa would help manage the cleaning staff. She loved the idea of being around students, so she took the job. But since she could not find a job there for her husband, she moved back to Detroit after one year.

Rosa returned to volunteering with the NAACP. But she needed a job that paid money, too. So she found work as a seamstress in a clothing factory. There she made a new friend, Elaine Steele. Still in high school, Elaine was much younger than Rosa. But the two women would stay good friends for life.

Rosa moved to Detroit and continued to speak about civil rights.

Marching for Change

Rosa also kept in touch with Dr. Martin Luther King, Jr. He helped inspire Rosa to keep fighting for civil rights. In 1963, when King practiced his famous "I Have a Dream" speech in Detroit, Rosa was at his side. She then traveled to the nation's capital to see him deliver the speech. King spoke at the March on Washington on August 28 before hundreds of thousands of people.

Rosa and the other women civil rights leaders there were not allowed to give speeches. They weren't even allowed to march alongside the men. They had a separate procession. Civil rights leader Bayard Rustin introduced Rosa to the crowd. He said she was a woman who had made a difference in the civil rights struggle. To many Americans, Rosa symbolized dignity in the face of unfair treatment.

In 1965, Rosa took part in another march led by King. Thousands of people walked 50 miles in Alabama, from Selma to Montgomery, the capital. They marched to demand equal voting rights.

This was the second time they had tried to march to Montgomery. The first time, the marchers were attacked by state troopers and they had to turn back. The march took five days, and Rosa joined in for the final eight miles. When the march finally ended at the Montgomery capitol, there was a crowd of angry white people. A few months later, President Lyndon Johnson signed the Voting Rights Act, which made voting tests illegal. Still, there was a long way to go until all people were treated equally.

In 1965, Dr. Martin Luther King, Jr., leads a civil rights march in Alabama.

ROSA'S GIFT *to* US

In 1965, Rosa got an exciting new job. She became an assistant to a black U.S. congressman from Michigan named John Conyers. One of her responsibilities was to find housing for homeless people. Rosa felt good about

Rosa (center, in light-colored suit) was an honored guest at many events. In this picture, she takes part in a 1976 parade in Detroit, Michigan.

her position and the fact that she was helping others.

But the next several years were hard for Rosa. She lost many people who were important to her. In 1968, King was assassinated. Her husband died of cancer in 1977. Two years later, her mother also passed away. At the age of 66, Rosa moved into an apartment building for senior citizens. She was ready to begin the next chapter in her life.

Teens enjoyed meeting Rosa and talking to her about her life.

Making a Difference

Rosa kept working to make the nation a better place. She was employed by Congressman Conyers until she was 75 years old. But Rosa wanted to do even more.

In 1987, Rosa created an organization called the Rosa and Raymond Parks Institute for Self Development. Elaine Steele helped her start the institute, which is still around today. It teaches teens about African-American history and assists them in finding jobs.

Together, Rosa and Elaine took the students on field trips. On one trip, they visited important places that had been part of the Underground Railroad. On another trip, Rosa took the teens to places that had been important in the civil rights movement. Many people around the country gave money to help pay for these trips.

As Rosa got older, her health declined. She could no longer travel, march, or make speeches. She had to stop running the Parks Institute and asked Elaine to take over for her. Rosa still struggled with money, but her friends helped her pay rent and other expenses.

Remembering a Heroine

The nation never forgot "the mother of the civil rights movement." All over the country, schools and streets were named for her. The Rosa Parks Library and Museum in Montgomery was built in her honor. Visitors can learn about her life there.

Rosa also received many important awards and honors. In 1996, President Bill Clinton awarded her the Presidential Medal of Freedom for her contributions to civil rights. Three years later, he presented Rosa with the Congressional Gold Medal, the highest honor the U.S. government can give.

On October 24, 2005, Rosa died in her Detroit apartment at the age of 92. Several close friends were

A proud Rosa received the Presidential Medal of Freedom from President Bill Clinton.

at her side. News of her death saddened the nation, and many people planned special ways to say goodbye. Hundreds of mourners attended a memorial in Montgomery, and thousands more celebrated Rosa's life at a service in Washington, D.C. For two days, Rosa's coffin was placed inside the U.S. Capitol so that people could pay their respects. This is a tradition usually saved for presidents and war heroes. Rosa was the first woman to receive this honor.

At the memorials, dozens of people spoke about Rosa's incredible life. Reverend Jesse Jackson, a civil rights leader and politician, gave a moving speech about Rosa. "Rosa Parks has shown the awesome power of right over might in history's long journey for peace and freedom," he said.

Thousands of Americans paid their respects to Rosa Parks in the U.S. Capitol.

Mourners at a memorial in Detroit, Michigan, thank Rosa for her contribution to the civil rights movement.

Rosa was laid to rest in a Detroit cemetery. She was buried next to her husband, mother, and brother. On the day of her funeral, flags all over the nation were flown at half-staff. In Montgomery, Detroit, and other cities, the front seats of city buses were left empty to represent the nation's loss.

Over the years, Rosa Parks has served as a role model for many Americans. By refusing to move from a seat on a bus, she stood up for what was fair and right. She showed that, with courage and determination, one person can change the world.

Key Dates in the Life of Rosa Parks

1913 — Born on February 4, in Tuskegee, Alabama

Moved to Montgomery, Alabama — 1924

1932 — Married Raymond Parks

Joined the NAACP — 1943

Refused to go to the — 1955
back of a bus and
was arrested, which
started a bus boycott   1956 — Sat in the front
                                                 of a bus after bus
                                                 segregation was ruled
Attended the March — 1963   unconstitutional
on Washington

Received the — 1999
Congressional
Gold Medal

2005 — Died on October 24,
          in Detroit, Michigan

Barack Obama

First African-American President

BLESSED

When the baby was born on August 4, 1961, in Honolulu, Hawaii, no one could have guessed that he would live such a remarkable life. Still, he was given a promising name: Barack, an African name that means "blessed." The baby was named for his father, Barack Obama, Sr., who was from Kenya.

Young Barack went by the nickname Barry when he was young. Although it certainly wasn't clear at the time, he would grow into his promising name. He would become a magnetic speaker and a talented politician. He would inspire hope and change, and he would one day become the first African-American president of the United States.

Barack Obama in 2008

Barry, age 2, with his mother, Ann Dunham

Strong Mother

Barry's mother had an unusual name, too. Her parents had named her Stanley, after her father, because they had wanted a boy. As a child, she went by Stanley, but later she used her middle name, Ann. Stanley Ann Dunham was a quiet and studious girl with a bold streak. She later traveled halfway around the world to study anthropology. In 1960, she was living with her parents in Hawaii, where they had moved after she graduated from high school. She attended the University of Hawaii. There she met and later married Barack Obama, Sr.

Barry's father had a booming voice and a brilliant mind. He was also ambitious. When little Barry was not quite a year old, his father left Hawaii to study at

Barack Obama and his father during his father's only visit, in 1972

Harvard University in Cambridge, Massachusetts. His parents divorced two years later. Barry would see his father again only once, when he was 10 years old. His mother would be the strongest influence on him. As an adult, he wrote, "What is best in me I owe to her."

A New Start

After his father left, money was tight for Barry and his mother. His mother returned to school, and her parents watched Barry while she was studying. At college, she met another foreign student, Lolo Soetoro.

The Soetoro family: (from left) stepfather Lolo, mother Ann, half sister Maya, Barry

He was easygoing and happily devoted hours to playing chess with Ann's father and wrestling with Barry. Lolo and Ann were married in 1965, and he returned to his home in Jakarta, Indonesia.

Ann and 6-year-old Barry spent months preparing to follow his new stepfather to Indonesia. They got passports and vaccinations to protect them from tropical diseases. Until then, neither had left the country. After a long journey, they landed in an unrecognizable place.

INDONESIA

Lolo's house was on the outskirts of Jakarta. It was a long way from the high-rises of Honolulu. There was no electricity, and the streets were not paved. Two baby crocodiles, along with chickens and birds-of-paradise, were in the backyard. Ann and Barry were the first foreigners to live in the neighborhood. To get to know the kids next door, Barry sat on a wall between their houses and flapped his arms like a great big bird, making cawing noises. "That got the kids laughing, and then they all played together," remembers Kay Ikranagara, a friend.

Barry attended a Catholic school called St. Francis of Assisi. He was sometimes teased because he looked different from the other kids. For one thing, he was the only black student at the school. He was also chubbier than the locals. But he seemed to shrug off the teasing, eating tofu and tempeh, picking guavas off trees, and playing soccer like the other kids.

Burning the Midnight Oil

Barry's mother taught him that education was important. Every day, she woke him at 4 a.m. to give him English lessons. She couldn't afford the elite international school and worried he wasn't challenged enough. After two years at the Catholic school, Barry moved to a state-run elementary school. He was the only foreigner, says Ati Kisjanto, a classmate, but he spoke some Indonesian and made new friends.

Worried that there weren't many black role models in her son's life, Barry's mother tried to provide them through books and music. At night, she came home from work with books on the civil rights movement

SDN Menteng 01 in Jakarta, Indonesia, where Barry attended elementary school

and recordings of Mahalia Jackson. "She believed that people were all basically the same under their skin," Barack later said in an interview, "that bigotry of any sort was wrong and that the goal was then to treat everybody as unique individuals."

Mahalia Jackson

Hard Choices

When Barack was 10 years old, his grandparents helped get a scholarship for him to attend an elite prep school in Hawaii called Punahou. He returned to Hawaii to live with them.

Barack went to the Punahou School in Honolulu, Hawaii, from 1971 to 1979.

A year later, his mother and half sister, Maya, followed. But after three years of living with her children in a small apartment in Honolulu, Barack's mother decided to go back to Indonesia to do fieldwork for her PhD. Barack, then about 14, stayed behind when his mother and sister left.

Barack lived with his grandparents throughout his teens. He struggled in those years to figure out where he fit in. At Punahou, he was one of only seven or eight black students. He was frustrated by the assumptions his classmates made about him. At the same time, he was terrified by a sense of not belonging.

Left: Barack plays basketball with the Punahou School team in 1979. He would continue to play basketball throughout his life—even in the White House.

Right: Barack and a classmate process down the aisle at his high school graduation in 1979.

Barack Obama celebrates his high school graduation with his grandparents.

"I learned to slip back and forth between my black and white worlds . . . ," he later wrote, "convinced that with a bit of translation on my part the two worlds would eventually [come together]."

STARTING OUT

After high school, Obama attended Occidental College, in Los Angeles, California, and Columbia University in New York City. He graduated from Columbia with a degree in political science in 1983. Then he moved to Chicago, Illinois, to be a community organizer, encouraging people to work together for positive change in their neighborhoods. Obama held meetings at Altgeld Gardens, a public housing project that serves a poor community. He worked with people there to advocate, or speak up, for their community. He got a new job intake center opened in the neighborhood. But he wanted to do more.

Barack, at Harvard Law School, poses with a copy of the *Harvard Law Review*.

Back to School

In 1988, Obama went to Harvard Law School. He studied constitutional law and worked as a research assistant. Even then, he showed the qualities that would lead him to the White House. His adviser, Laurence Tribe, later said, "I've known senators, presidents. I've never known anyone with what seems to me more raw political talent. He just seems to have the surest way of calmly reaching across what are impenetrable barriers to many people." In 1990, Obama was the first African American to be elected president of the *Harvard Law Review*. After his first year at Harvard, he spent a summer working for a top law firm in Chicago, where he met Michelle Robinson.

Finding Happiness

Michelle had a more traditional upbringing than Barack, having grown up in a modest two-parent home on Chicago's South Side. He later said that her stability appealed to him. When Obama graduated from law school in 1991, he turned down higher-paying offers from big law firms and joined a small civil rights firm in Chicago. In 1992, Barack and Michelle were married.

Barack and Michelle celebrate Christmas together in Hawaii.

A Career in Politics

Obama during his time as a state senator, 2002

Never one to sit still, Obama focused on moving his career into politics. In 1995, he wrote a book, *Dreams from My Father*, about his experiences growing up. A year later, he ran for the Illinois state senate and won.

Over the next years, both his family and his career grew. In 1998, his first child, Malia Ann, was born, and he was reelected to a second term in the state senate. His second daughter, Natasha "Sasha" Obama, was born in 2001.

Bitter Disappointment

In 2000, Obama tried to break out of state government and into national politics. He ran for a seat in the U.S. House of Representatives. His opponent in the primary election was a four-term U.S. congressman named

Representative Bobby Rush celebrates his victory over Barack Obama in 2000.

Bobby Rush. Rush was a former member of the Black Panthers, a party that had advocated forcefully for African-American rights in the 1960s and 1970s. He ridiculed Obama as a Harvard-educated outsider. Obama was soundly defeated—Rush got twice as many votes.

But Obama did not give up. He put his dreams of national politics on hold for a while and ran again for the Illinois state senate in 2002. He began to get some national attention after he gave a strong speech opposing the Iraq War. In the Illinois senate, he worked to pass laws to help protect civil rights. Similar bills had failed before. But Obama showed a skill that would serve him well throughout his career: figuring out how to present his case positively and win over opponents.

Sudden Stardom

But it was the 2004 Democratic National Convention that gave Obama the national spotlight. In Boston, Massachusetts, on the night of July 27, he delivered a moving convention speech. Facing thousands of Democrats, he described a country that America wanted very badly to be: a country that was not driven by racism and fear. He described a place in which an African immigrant could marry a midwestern white woman, and their middle-class son could go to Harvard Law School and run for political office. "In no other

Obama captures the nation's attention during the Democratic National Convention on July 27, 2004.

On November 2, 2004, the Obamas watched election returns together for news of whether Barack had won a seat in the U.S. Senate.

country on Earth," he said, "is my story even possible."

Obama's speech mesmerized people because he seemed to speak for many, black and white, immigrant and native born. Three months later, he was elected to the U.S. Senate from Illinois.

SENATOR OBAMA

In January 2005, Barack Obama became the only African American in the U.S. Senate. In fact, in the previous 100 years, there had been only two other black senators. Six feet one inch tall and always impeccably dressed, Obama was charming and intense. He won people over with a combination of humility and confidence. "I probably always feel on some level I can persuade anybody I talk to," Obama told TIME magazine.

Obama in Washington, D.C., in 2008

Before he ever cast a vote in the Senate, some were already declaring he would be the first black president. That kind of fame can be awkward in the Senate—where nearly every member thinks he or she could be president. But Obama won over other Democrats by paying respect to their experience.

Republicans also embraced Obama, realizing that any legislation he co-sponsored would get more attention. As a result, Obama was able to get more done in his first year than a new senator normally could. He joined an effort to prepare for outbreaks of avian flu. He helped get more money for veterans' health care. Obama's Republican opponents undoubtedly worried that his political future might be *too* promising—they knew he would be hard to beat as a presidential contender.

Barack Obama was part of a new generation of black leaders who insisted on being seen as more than representatives of their race. His African-American roots were very important to him. Photos of Muhammad Ali and Dr. Martin Luther King, Jr., adorned his office walls, along with a painting of Thurgood Marshall, the first black Supreme Court justice. But he saw no need to be a black leader on all issues. "I don't know who the top white leader is," he said. He aspired to be a leader for all people.

NUCLEAR ROGUES & HOW TO CONTROL THEM | CLINT'S TAKE ON HEROES

TIME

Why Barack Obama Could Be **The Next U.S. President**

By Joe Klein

Plus: An exclusive excerpt from the Senator's book

www.timecanada.com

Early in Obama's Senate career, many people were already predicting he would be president. This is a TIME magazine cover from October 23, 2006.

THE ROAD
to the
WHITE HOUSE

On February 10, 2007, Barack Obama announced that he was running for president. As a 45-year-old first-term U.S. senator, he was an unlikely candidate. He was young and relatively inexperienced.

For the location of his announcement, Obama chose the steps of the Old State Capitol building in Springfield, Illinois. Abraham Lincoln gave an important speech there in 1858, when he accepted his party's nomination to run for the U.S. Senate.

Obama acknowledged his lack of experience. He told the crowd, "I know I haven't spent a lot of time learning

Obama at the Old State Capitol in Springfield, Illinois, on February 4, 2007

the ways of Washington, but I've been there long enough to know that the ways of Washington must change." His main Democratic rival in the presidential primaries was U.S. senator Hillary Clinton. They both campaigned hard, and after the primaries on June 3, 2008, Obama had won 2,159 delegates to Clinton's 1,920. Clinton was out of the race a few days later.

Running for President

In the summer of a presidential election year, both political parties gather their members for national conventions. The 2008 Democratic National Convention was held in Denver, Colorado, from August 25 to August 28. After speeches by Michelle Obama, Hillary Clinton, former president Bill Clinton, and other important politicians, Barack Obama was formally named the Democratic Party's candidate for president. U.S. senator Joe Biden was introduced as

Obama chose Joe Biden (in background) as his running mate.

Barack Obama's running mate on the final night of the convention. They would face Republican senator John McCain, from Arizona, and his running mate, Alaska governor Sarah Palin, in the general election.

In the few months between the national conventions and the general election, Obama and McCain traveled the country. They gave speeches, raised money, and told voters what they would do if they became president.

Obama's slogan was, "Yes, We Can!" He spoke about changing energy policies, improving the health-care system, cutting taxes for many Americans, and creating more affordable housing, among other issues.

His campaign also used the Internet in new ways to share information and organize volunteers. By Election Day, his campaign had an e-mail list of about 13 million addresses.

Attendees at the Democratic National Convention cheer after Obama accepted the nomination for president on August 28, 2008. From left are Michelle Obama, Jill Biden, Malia Obama, Sasha Obama, Barack Obama, and Joe Biden.

Moment of Truth

On Tuesday, November 4, 2008, 61.6% of eligible voters went to the polls to vote for their next president. When American voters cast their ballots for president, they are voting for members of the Electoral College, rather than a particular candidate. Each state has a set number of electoral votes based on population. To win the presidency, a candidate must receive at least 270 of the 538 possible electoral votes. Barack Obama won 365 electoral votes, and more than 69 million votes from Americans.

Victory

On Election Night, Barack Obama climbed onto a stage in Grant Park, Chicago, in front of hundreds of thousands of supporters. Michelle, 7-year-old Sasha, and 10-year-old Malia joined him onstage. He gave a soaring speech that acknowledged how unlikely it had been that someone with his background would win the election, saying: "If there is anyone out there who still doubts that America is a place where all things are possible, who still wonders if the dream of our founders is alive in our time, who still questions the power of our democracy, tonight is your answer."

The Obamas celebrate their victory in Grant Park on November 4, 2008.

He also reminded his followers that he would have a lot of hard work to do as president: "There will be setbacks and false starts. There are many who won't agree with every decision or policy I make as president, and we know the government can't solve every problem. But I will always be honest with you about the challenges we face. I will listen to you, especially when we disagree. And above all, I will ask you to join in the work of remaking this nation the only way it's been done in America for 221 years— block by block, brick by brick, calloused hand by calloused hand."

Obama is sworn in as president on January 20, 2009.

Making History

On January 20, 2009, Barack Obama became the first African-American president in U.S. history. He took the oath of office using the same Bible that Abraham Lincoln had used when he was sworn in as president on March 4, 1861. Lincoln had led the country through the Civil War and issued the Emancipation Proclamation, which gave slaves the legal status of freed people. Just four decades before Obama's Inauguration, black citizens had been prevented from voting. Now a black American recited the oath of office and delivered an Inaugural speech. Though it was a cold winter day, almost 2 million visitors flooded the nation's capital, and millions more tuned in to TVs, radios, and computers worldwide to witness the historic event.

Moving In

Like other First Families before them, the Obamas moved into the White House on Inauguration Day. Members of the White House staff had about five hours to remove the last of the previous presidential family's belongings and unload and unpack the Obamas' things. When the Obamas returned from the Inauguration parade around 5 p.m., they were officially home.

YES, WE DID IT!

In the White House, Barack and Michelle Obama worked hard to make sure Malia and Sasha lived a normal life. They wanted their daughters to learn responsibility, and insisted that the girls pick up after themselves and make their own beds, even though they had a staff who would do it for them. Michelle's mother, Marian Robinson, helped with the girls when their parents attended events.

As president, Obama worked to improve the nation's economy. He took office during an economic recession. Many people were out of work, companies were failing, and Americans were struggling. It was also a time of division in politics. Republicans took control of Congress, which made it difficult for Obama and the

The Obama family heads to church in 2010.

Democrats to make the changes they wanted. Still, Obama was elected to a second term in 2012.

Big Changes

By the time Obama left office, the unemployment rate was 4.9%—an improvement from when he entered office. The value of stock on the stock market had tripled. Although many challenges remained, by many measures the U.S. economy had bounced back from the recession.

Obama also sought to make progress on U.S. relationships with other nations. In January 2016, after a long negotiation, Iran agreed to a deal that would keep it from producing dangerous nuclear weapons. In March of that same year, Obama became the first U.S. president since 1928 to visit Cuba. Located just 90 miles off the coast of Florida, Cuba has for many years been at odds with the U.S. The trip was a sign of an improving relationship.

Obama also took important steps to help the environment. During his presidency, the U.S. was among the 175 nations to sign the Paris Agreement. The agreement lays out a plan for countries around the globe to work together against climate change.

But he will probably be most remembered for a law that he championed in his first years in office: the

Obama, with Sasha (left) and Malia (right), pardons a turkey in 2015.

Affordable Care Act. Although it was far from perfect, the law made it possible for millions of Americans who had not been able to get health insurance to receive it.

Saying Goodbye

On January 10, 2017, Obama delivered one last speech as president. Looking back on his eight years in office, he thanked the people who had helped him during his time in the White House. "I leave this stage tonight even more optimistic about this country than when we started," Obama concluded. "Because I know our work has not only helped so many Americans, it has inspired so many Americans—especially so many young people out there—to believe that you can make a difference."

Finally, Obama assured Americans that he would spend the rest of his life working alongside them to make a difference. As he stepped away from the podium, Obama spoke some familiar words: "Yes, we can. Yes, we did. Yes, we can."

The Obamas during Barack's campaign for reelection, September 7, 2012

Key Dates in the Life of Barack Obama

1961 — Born August 4, in Honolulu, Hawaii

Graduated from Columbia University with a degree in political science; became a community organizer in Chicago, Illinois — 1983

1991 — Graduated from Harvard Law School

Married Michelle Robinson — 1992

Became an Illinois ●——— **1996**
state senator

2004——● Gave a speech at the
Democratic National
Convention; elected
Elected president of ●——— **2008**   to U.S. Senate
the United States

Reelected president ●——— **2012**
of the United States

2017 ——● Left office

Heroes

Harriet Tubman, Jackie Robinson, Rosa Parks, and Barack Obama are all inspiring figures in the fight for civil rights. Black history is filled with many great heroes. You can learn more of their stories by diving into the biographies of these pioneers.

Maya Angelou
(1928–2014)

Maya Angelou was a poet, a nonfiction writer, a civil rights activist, and an inspiration to many. She is most known for her book *I Know Why the Caged Bird Sings*. The book describes some of Angelou's experiences growing up in a segregated part of the South. She wrote several other books about her life and also published collections of her poetry.

Louis Armstrong
(1901–1971)

Louis Armstrong was born in New Orleans, Louisiana, on August 4, 1901. As a child, he learned to play the cornet. He loved it! He decided to make music his life. Armstrong went on to record thousands of songs. He was best known for playing the trumpet and singing. He also acted in more than 20 movies. Today, Armstrong's home, in New York City, is a museum.

Ruby Bridges
(1954–)

On November 14, 1960, Ruby Bridges, then 6, became the first black student to attend an all-white elementary school in the South. U.S. Marshals had to protect Ruby from angry protesters. Years later, she wrote, "I learned many things . . . that year, but the primary lesson was the same one that Martin Luther King tried to teach all of us: never judge people by the color of their skin."

George Washington Carver
(1860s–1943)

George Washington Carver was an inventor, a botanist, and a teacher. He is best known for creating more than 325 products from peanuts. Born into slavery in Missouri, he grew up to attend what is now known as Iowa State University. He later taught at the Tuskegee Institute, in Alabama.

Shirley Chisholm
(1924–2005)

Shirley Chisholm was an influential voice in Congress for 14 years. In 1968, she was elected to Congress from New York City. In 1972, she became the first African American to seek the Democratic presidential nomination. Chisholm described her approach to life by saying, "You don't make progress by standing on the sidelines, whimpering and complaining. You make progress by implementing ideas."

Frederick Douglass
(1818–1895)

Frederick Douglass was born into slavery in Talbot County, Maryland, and raised by his grandmother, who was a slave. Douglass learned to read, even though it was forbidden to teach slaves to read and write. When he was 20 years old, he escaped from slavery. He went on to publish the antislavery newspaper the *North Star*, and helped hundreds of people find their way to freedom.

W.E.B. Du Bois
(1868–1963)

Author and activist W.E.B. Du Bois was an outspoken advocate of equal rights for women and African Americans. In 1895, he became the first African American to receive a PhD from Harvard University. He cofounded the National Association for the Advancement of Colored People in 1909, and went on to support African nations in their struggle for independence from European rule.

Althea Gibson
(1927–2003)

Althea Gibson was born in Silver, South Carolina. She was a professional tennis player and golfer. She faced much discrimination, as rules often prevented blacks and whites from playing on the same tennis courts. She was the first African-American player to play and win at top tennis tournaments, including Wimbledon and the U.S. Nationals (now called the U.S. Open).

Dorothy Height
(1912–2010)

Born on March 24, 1912, in Richmond, Virginia, Dorothy Height was an activist who fought for equal rights for African Americans and for women. For more than 40 years, she served as president of the National Council of Negro Women, a group that works to improve opportunities and life for African-American women and their families.

Matthew Henson
(1866–1955)

Born in Maryland, Matthew Henson grew up to be an adventurous spirit and the first black Arctic explorer. He made several expeditions to the Arctic with Commander Robert Peary, reaching the North Pole in 1909. In 1912, he wrote a book about his adventures, *A Negro Explorer at the North Pole*.

Langston Hughes
(1902–1967)

Langston Hughes was a poet whose writing expressed the experience of working-class African Americans. He used the rhythm of jazz and of everyday speech in his poetry. Sometimes called the "Poet Laureate of Harlem," Hughes was a central figure in the Harlem Renaissance.

Jesse Jackson
(1941–)

Born in 1941 in Greenville, South Carolina, Jesse Jackson was a member of the Southern Christian Leadership Conference (SCLC) who worked closely with Dr. Martin Luther King, Jr. After King's death, Jackson became an ordained minister and founded the Rainbow PUSH coalition, a civil rights group. Jackson ran for the Democratic nomination for president in 1984 and 1988. He received 6.7 million votes in the 1988 primaries, putting him solidly in third place. Jackson's two campaigns showed the key role black people play in national politics. Today, Jackson remains one of the nation's best-known political leaders.

Coretta Scott King
(1927–2006)

Coretta Scott King was an activist for civil rights for African Americans and women. After her husband, Dr. Martin Luther King, Jr., was assassinated in 1968, King dedicated her life to pursuing his dream of ending racism and poverty in the United States. She founded the Martin Luther King, Jr., Center for Nonviolent Social Change. King also led the effort to establish a national holiday in her husband's name.

Dr. Martin Luther King, Jr.
(1929–1968)

Dr. Martin Luther King, Jr., was born in Atlanta, Georgia. When he was a child, unfair laws kept black people and white people apart. King worked to change those laws. He spoke about how all people should be treated fairly. He taught peaceful protest and inspired tens of thousands to march for civil rights. His "I Have a Dream" speech, delivered at the March on Washington in 1963, remains an inspiration to this day.

John Lewis
(1940–)

As a young man, John Lewis was inspired to fight for civil rights while listening to radio broadcasts by Dr. Martin Luther King, Jr. From 1963 to 1966, Lewis led the Student Nonviolent Coordinating Committee, a group that organized sit-ins, marches, and freedom rides protesting segregation in the South. He helped organize the March on Washington. He has been a U.S. representative for Georgia since 1987 and continues to be a powerful voice for civil rights.

Jesse Owens
(1913–1980)

In 1936, the Olympics were held in Berlin, Germany. Nazi-party leader Adolf Hitler aimed to use the games to showcase what he believed was the superiority of his people. Hitler considered black people inferior to whites. With grace under pressure and a superstar performance, Jesse Owens, the son of a sharecropper and the grandson of slaves, proved Hitler wrong. He won four gold medals and set three world records in track and field. "The battles that count aren't the ones for gold medals [but] the struggles within yourself," Owens later said.

Ida B. Wells
(1862–1931)

Ida B. Wells was a journalist and activist for equal rights. Orphaned at the age of 16, she attended college at Shaw University. She was one of the first women in the U.S. to keep her maiden name when she married. A founding member of the NAACP, she was also a gifted public speaker who traveled the country speaking about the need for equal rights and women's suffrage, or voting rights.

Granville T. Woods
(1856–1910)

Granville T. Woods was born in Columbus, Ohio. The African-American inventor was known as the "Black Edison." His many inventions and accomplishments include helping develop the telephone and a system known as the induction telegraph, which allowed moving trains to communicate. He also invented the electrified "third rail" that is still used to power trains in subway systems today.

Malcolm X
(1925–1965)

During the early 1960s, Malcolm X gained recognition as the spokesperson for the Nation of Islam, a political and religious group that promoted black superiority and self-dependence. Malcolm X spoke out forcefully against the unfair treatment of African Americans and encouraged them to use "any means necessary," including violence, to achieve equality. In 1964, he traveled to Mecca, in Saudi Arabia. It is the most holy city of Muslims. Inspired by his pilgrimage, Malcolm X left the Nation of Islam and changed his views, choosing a more peaceful route to accomplish his goals. On February 21, 1965, He was shot and killed in New York City by Nation members who did not agree with his new ideas.

Glossary

abolitionist
A person who worked to abolish, or end, slavery before the Civil War.

advocate
To support or argue for.

assassinate
To murder an important or well-known person.

bail
Money paid for the release of a prisoner accused of a crime. If the accused person shows up for trial as he or she promised to, the bail is returned.

bias
A tendency to support or reject a particular person or group, often based on unfair or untrue reasoning.

bigotry
The treatment of the members of a specific group with hatred and prejudice.

botanist
A scientist who studies plant life.

boycott
A refusal to engage with a person, organization, or business, as a form of protest or punishment.

campaign
A plan of action to achieve a certain goal. Candidates for office run campaigns to convince people to vote for them.

candidate
A person who is running for office in an election or applying for a job.

car pool
A system in which a group of people travel together by car.

civil rights
The rights to freedom and equal treatment guaranteed to all citizens in a democracy.

convention
A meeting of people for a particular purpose. Political parties hold conventions to choose their candidates for office.

delegate
A person who represents other people at a convention. Delegates at political conventions vote on who they want their candidates for office to be.

demonstration
A public protest by a group of people.

discrimination
The unfair treatment of people based on their race or other characteristics.

drafted
To be made to serve in the military.

economy
The system of producing, selling, and buying things and services in a society, and of managing its money.

fieldwork
Work done in a specific environment in order to learn through personal observation and experience.

humility
The quality of being modest, not proud, and able to recognize one's own mistakes.

immigrant
A person who moves to live in another country.

impenetrable
Unable to be crossed or broken through.

inauguration
A ceremony during which a person officially takes a public job.

integrated
Not separated by race or any other characteristic.

integrity
The quality of being honest, trustworthy, and moral.

Jim Crow law
A law that discriminates against black people, often by keeping them separate from white people.

legislation
Laws that have been suggested or made official.

lingo
A special language.

march
A group of people walking together to support or protest something.

mesmerize
To dazzle; to hypnotize.

nationalism
Pride in and loyalty to one's country (or other group). A black nationalist supports separating from whites and forming black communities that rule themselves.

negotiation
The process of discussing and compromising to reach an agreement.

nomination
The process of suggesting someone as a candidate for a job.

overseer
A person who is in charge of other people. Before the Civil War, overseers were in charge of slaves.

persuade
To change someone's mind by giving him or her good reasons to do so; to convince.

pilgrimage
A trip to a holy place.

plantation
A large farm. Before the Civil War, many slaves worked on plantations in the South, where they were held captive by their owners.

pneumonia
A serious disease in which the lungs fill with a thick liquid, making breathing difficult.

political science
The study of government.

prejudice
An unfair opinion or untrue belief about someone based on that person's race or other characteristic.

primary
An election in which voters choose a candidate to represent a certain political party in a later election against candidates of other parties.

protest
A public statement against something.

racist
Believing that one particular race is superior to other races.

ratify
To approve officially.

recession
A period when business slows down in an area.

During a recession, many workers may lose their jobs.

remedy
A medicine or treatment that eases pain or cures a disease.

renaissance
A period of increased interest in knowledge and the arts; a rebirth or revival.

reservoir
A human-made lake where water is collected and stored for later use.

resolution
An official statement of opinion, voted on by a group.

ridicule
To make fun of.

running mate
A person who runs for office alongside another candidate, in a less important role. When a person is elected president, his or her running mate becomes vice president.

scholarship
Money given to help pay for schooling.

scout
A person who is sent out to bring back information. As a Civil War scout, Harriet Tubman learned information about enemy soldiers and shared it with the Union army. Baseball scouts search for people who might be good at playing professional baseball.

segregated
Separated by race or some other characteristic, or restricted to members of one group. Segregated schools are open to students of only one race.

sharecropper
A farmer who rents land that belongs to someone else. The sharecropper pays the owner with a portion of the harvest.

sit-in
A demonstration in which people protest something by sitting on the floor of an establishment, or in the seats of a place where they are not permitted.

slave
A person who is owned by another person and forced to work for that person for no pay.

sponsor
To suggest and support a proposed law.

stock market
The network through which a person can invest money in and own small parts of various businesses.

suffrage
The right to vote.

unconstitutional
Against the laws and basic principles described in the Constitution.

upbringing
The care a child receives while growing up.

vaccination
A dose of medicine that protects against a specific disease.

white supremacy
The belief that white people are better than people of other races and that white people should have control over other races.

Index

Picture Credits

176: Michael Ngan/AFP/Getty Images; **179:** Chip Somodevilla/Getty Images; **181:** Saul Loeb/AFP/Getty Images; **182:** Splash News; **183:** (from top) Chip Somodevilla/Getty Images, Saul Loeb/AFP/Getty Images; **184:** (top to bottom, left to right) Edward A. Hausner/New York Times Co./Getty Images, Gilles Petard/Redferns/Getty Images, Frederick M. Brown/Getty Images, Universal History Archive/UIG/Getty Images, NY Daily News Archive/Getty Images, Fotosearch/Getty Images; **185:** (top to bottom, left to right) Universal History Archive/Getty Images, Authenticated News/Archive Photos/Getty Images, Express Newspapers/Getty Images, Apic/Getty Images, Underwood Archives/Getty Images, Mickey Adair/Getty Images, Michael Evans/New York Times Co./Getty Images **186:** (top to bottom, left to right) Photo12/UIG/Getty Images, Jeff Hutchens/Getty Images, ullstein bild/Getty Images, Universal History Archive/UIG/Getty images, Kean Collection/Getty Images, Photo12/UIG/Getty Images.

Acknowledgments

Editor, TIME For Kids: Nellie Gonzalez Cutler
Senior Editor, TIME For Kids: Elizabeth Winchester

Executive Editor: Beth Sutinis
Editor: Deirdre Langeland
Art Director: Georgia Morrissey
Designer: Dirk Kaufman
Photo Researcher: Katherine Bourbeau
Production Manager: Hillary Leary
Prepress Manager: Alex Voznesenskiy

The Harriet Tubman biography was previously published as *TIME For Kids: Harriet Tubman: A Woman of Courage* by the Editors of TIME For Kids with Renée Skelton, HarperCollins, 2005.

The Jackie Robinson biography was previously published as *TIME For Kids: Jackie Robinson: Strong Inside and Out* by the Editors of TIME For Kids with Denise Lewis Patrick, HarperCollins, 2005.

The Rosa Parks biography was previously published as *TIME For Kids: Rosa Parks: Civil Rights Pioneer* by the Editors of TIME For Kids with Karen Kellaher, HarperCollins, 2007.

Portions of the Barack Obama biography were previously published as follows:

Amanda Ripley, "A Mother's Story," TIME magazine, April 21, 2008.

Amanda Ripley, "Obama's Ascent," TIME magazine, November 15, 2004.

Perry Bacon, Jr., "The Exquisite Dilemma of Being Obama," TIME magazine, February 20, 2006.

Amanda Ripley, "The Family Obama," TIME magazine, September 1, 2008.

TIME For Kids: President Obama: A Day in the Life of America's Leader by the Editors of TIME For Kids, TIME For Kids, 2009.

"Barack Obama: Person of the Year," TIME For Kids online, *timeforkids.com*, December 6, 2016.